The Ominous Struggle: Is It Really Beautiful?

GEORGE BEASLEY

Dedication

To all of us in the ominous struggle. Whatever that looks like, the struggle wants you to quit! Don't ever quit! You have a purpose in this world. Those who read this book may it for all time change your life and give you the hope to make it another day.

To the mental health crisis that we are in right now and time forever. It will never get better but only manageable. Depend on God putting the right people at the right time in your path to help you through your struggle.

To my wonderful Sweet Lisa who has fought for us in each and every ominous struggle and every beautiful struggle. Her love for me has added years to my life and made my struggle beautiful.

To my daughters, Laura and Sara, my grandchildren, Lincoln, Liam, Luke, Solomon, and Shepherd, and my son in loves, Justin and Allen: You have been the catalyst that has brought many changes in my life because of the unconditional love you have shown me over the years. You allowed me to journey at my pace and accepted me for the person I am.

To the wonderful people in the mental health profession, you are making a difference and I am proof of that. To my beautiful friend and therapist, Anne, who has made a profound impact on my life and on humanity itself. Her words at each and eve meeting brought new focus and a new prospective to any given struggle be it ominous or beautiful.

Most of all to the One who has seen me through each and every struggle and that is my God, who promises to take care of me through each and every storm. He has guided me and given me the hope necessary to take on the next struggle. He will never give up on you. He is my Lord and Savior who had sent for me and who has rescued me. In the end, it does matter.

Author's Note

Hello! I'm George Watson Beasley, an author and storyteller shaped by life's unseen challenges and triumphs. Born in Baltimore, Maryland, I've walked a path filled with struggles, revelations, and growth—experiences that ultimately led me to write *The Invisible Soul: Rise Up*.

This book is more than a story; it's a piece of my heart. It reflects my journey through fear, guilt, and self-doubt, revealing how these hidden forces shaped my life. For years, I carried the weight of silent struggles, masking my pain. Writing this book allowed me to unearth and embrace the invisible soul that has guided me through it all—a concept that resonates with many who've felt unseen or unheard.

Publishing this work wasn't without its challenges. The first edition faced setbacks under Tate Publishing, but I refused to let those obstacles define my story. Through faith and persistence, I partnered with Christian Faith Publishing to bring *The Invisible Soul* to life, adding even more depth and personal insight along the way.

This journey has taught me the importance of authenticity and the power of perseverance. I'm passionate about protecting the integrity of my work and using my experiences to encourage others to rise above the destructive forces that seek to hold them back. My hope is that my story inspires you to find strength in your own invisible soul and embrace the power of transformation.

Preface

In a world rife with challenges, we often find ourselves grappling with the complexities of existence. *The Ominous Struggle: Is It Really Beautiful?* is a journey through the myriad forms of struggle that define our lives. It is an exploration of what it means to face adversity in its many guises—be it personal, societal, or existential—and a reflection on the lessons learned along the way.

Life's struggles can feel isolating and overwhelming, yet they are universal experiences that transcend the boundaries of background, belief, and circumstance. This book seeks to illuminate the often-unspoken realities of struggle, starting from the personal battles we face within ourselves to the broader societal challenges that shape our lives. Each chapter delves into a different aspect of this struggle, inviting readers to reflect on their own experiences and consider the transformative power of hope, faith, and resilience.

The journey through this book will also confront the complexities of human relationships and societal expectations. From the struggles of transparency and vulnerability to the impact of judgment from peers, each chapter aims to foster empathy and understanding. In an age where materialism and the facade of happiness often overshadow authentic emotional expression, I invite readers to reconsider their values and find fulfillment beyond the superficial.

This book is a labor of love, borne from my own experiences and observations, and it is my sincerest hope that it resonates with you. May it serve as a companion for anyone grappling with their struggles, offering a sense of connection and encouragement in the pursuit of a life that, despite its challenges, can still be beautiful. Together, let us embark on this exploration of the ominous struggle, seeking not just understanding but also a deeper appreciation for the complexities of our shared humanity.

Contents

CHAPTER ONE

THE STRUGGLE DEFINED

"We are hard pressed on every side, but not crushed; perplexed, but not in despair; persecuted, but not abandoned; struck down, but not destroyed."

– 2 Corinthians 4:8-9

Life is a journey marked by countless trials and tribulations, often referred to simply as "the struggle." Understanding the complexities of the struggle is the first step toward overcoming it and achieving personal growth and spiritual fulfillment. Let us delve into the multifaceted nature of the struggle and explore the societal, personal, and existential challenges that shape our daily existence.

In today's fast-paced world, societal pressures are immense. We are constantly bombarded with expectations to achieve success, wealth, and social status. The media and social networks amplify these pressures, creating a distorted reality where comparison and competition thrive. Many find themselves trapped in a cycle of striving for external validation, losing sight of their true selves in the process. This struggle often leads to stress, anxiety, and a sense of unworthiness. It is essential to recognize that societal pressures, while pervasive, do not define our worth or dictate our potential for happiness. By shifting our focus from external validation to internal growth, we can begin to break free from the chains of societal struggle.

On a more intimate level, personal struggles are the battles we face within ourselves. These challenges are deeply personal and vary from person to person. They include our fears, insecurities, and doubts, as well as the wounds and traumas from our past. Personal struggles often stem from childhood experiences, shaping our beliefs and behaviors in adulthood.

For some, personal struggle is an internal war against self-sabotaging thoughts and limiting beliefs. For others, it is a fight against the pain of past traumas and the quest for healing and wholeness. Dealing with personal struggle requires courage and vulnerability, as it involves confronting the darkest parts of ourselves. However, it is through this confrontation that we find the path to true self-discovery and healing.

Beyond societal and personal struggles lies existential struggle, a profound and universal quest for meaning and purpose. This struggle touches the very core of our being, prompting us to ask questions about our existence and our place in the world. What is the purpose of life? Why do we suffer? What happens after we die? These questions have plagued humanity for centuries, and the search for answers is a fundamental aspect of the human experience.

Existential struggle often leads to a spiritual journey, where we seek to connect with something greater than ourselves. For many, this journey is guided by faith and the teachings of Religion. It is in our relationship with God that we find solace and understanding, realizing that our struggles are not in vain but part of a greater divine plan.

While the struggle is an inherent part of life, it is not without purpose. It is through the struggle that we grow, learn, and evolve. Embracing the struggle means acknowledging its presence and allowing it to be a catalyst for change. It means trusting in God's plan and having faith that every challenge we face is an opportunity for spiritual and personal growth.

As we navigate the societal, personal, and existential struggles, we are reminded of the words of Romans 5:3-4: *"We also glory in our sufferings, because we know that suffering produces perseverance; perseverance, character; and character, hope."* In our struggles, we find the strength to persevere, the character to overcome, and the hope to carry on.

It is a common misconception that struggle is limited to those with financial difficulties or those who lack social support. In truth, the struggle is a universal experience, transcending financial status, religious beliefs, and personal circumstances. Everyone, regardless of their background, faces challenges that test their strength, faith, and resilience.

For the wealthy, the struggle might manifest in ways that are less visible but equally profound. They may grapple with the pressure to maintain their status, the fear of losing their wealth, or the emptiness that can accompany material abundance without spiritual fulfillment. Wealth does not insulate one from the human condition; it merely shifts the nature of the challenges faced.

Similarly, those with strong religious beliefs are not exempt from struggle. Faith can provide immense comfort and guidance, but it can also be a source of internal conflict. Believers may wrestle with doubts, guilt, or the challenge of living up to their spiritual ideals. The struggle can be a crucible in which faith is tested and refined, ultimately leading to a deeper, more resilient spirituality.

Personal circumstances, too, shape the nature of the struggle. Each individual carries a unique set of experiences, traumas, and hopes. A person who has endured a difficult childhood may find the struggle rooted in overcoming past wounds and building a sense of self-worth. Another may face the struggle in the form of a debilitating illness, requiring strength and perseverance to navigate daily life.

Consider the story of Job from the Bible. Despite his righteousness and faithfulness, Job faced immense suffering—losing his wealth, his health, and his family. His story illustrates that struggle can strike anyone, regardless of their moral or spiritual standing. Yet, it is through his unwavering faith and endurance that Job ultimately finds restoration and a deeper understanding of God's purpose.

The universality of the struggle underscores a vital truth: no one is alone in their challenges. While the specifics of our struggles may differ, the underlying experience of facing hardship is something we all share. This shared experience can be a source of connection and empathy, reminding us that we are all part of the same human family.

Furthermore, recognizing that struggle is a common thread in the human experience allows us to approach others with greater compassion and understanding. It reminds us that the person next to us, regardless of their outward appearance of success or happiness, is also fighting their own battles. This perspective fosters a sense of community and support, encouraging us to lift each other up rather than judge or compete.

Moreover, understanding the universal nature of struggle helps us to be kinder to ourselves. It is easy to fall into the trap of thinking that we are uniquely burdened or that our struggles are a sign of personal failure. In reality, struggle is a testament to our humanity and a crucial part of our spiritual journey. Embracing this truth allows us to approach our challenges with grace and resilience.

As we move forward in this book, let us keep in mind that struggle is not a sign of weakness but a catalyst for growth. By embracing our struggles and viewing them as opportunities for personal and spiritual development, we can transform our hardships into stepping stones toward a more meaningful and fulfilling life. Together, we will explore the tools and insights needed to navigate these struggles with faith, courage, and hope, trusting that each challenge we face brings us one step closer to the divine purpose that God has set for us.

By acknowledging the myriad forms that struggle can take, we equip ourselves with a broader perspective and a deeper empathy for our own experiences and those of others.

The complexities of struggle are rooted in the diverse tapestry of human existence. Every individual's journey is shaped by a unique blend of factors—cultural background, family dynamics, personal experiences, and spiritual beliefs. These factors influence how we perceive and respond to the challenges that come our way. Understanding this diversity is crucial, as it prevents us from adopting a one-size-fits-all approach to struggle and encourages a more nuanced, compassionate perspective.

Consider the cultural aspect of the struggle. In some cultures, there is a strong emphasis on community and collective well-being, where personal struggles are shared and supported by the group. In other cultures, individualism is prized, and personal struggles are often faced alone, fostering resilience but also potentially leading to isolation. Recognizing these cultural differences helps us appreciate the varied ways people navigate their hardships and seek support.

Family dynamics also play a significant role in shaping our struggles. A person raised in a loving, supportive family may face different challenges compared to someone from a dysfunctional or abusive household. The former might struggle with external pressures, while the latter might grapple with deep-seated emotional wounds. Both experiences are valid and significant, and understanding these differences allows us to approach each individual's struggle with sensitivity and respect.

Personal experiences, including past traumas, achievements, and relationships, further add to the complexity of the struggle. A person who has experienced significant loss might struggle with grief and finding meaning in life, while someone who has achieved great success might struggle with the pressure to maintain that success and the fear of failure. These personal histories shape our responses to new challenges, influencing our resilience, coping mechanisms, and outlook on life.

Spiritual beliefs also provide a crucial lens through which we view our struggles. For many, faith is a source of strength and guidance, offering a sense of purpose and hope in the face of adversity. However, spiritual struggles can also arise, such as questioning one's faith during difficult times or reconciling religious teachings with personal experiences. Understanding the spiritual dimension of struggle is essential for providing holistic support and fostering spiritual growth.

By setting the foundation for understanding the complexities and diversity of struggles, we prepare ourselves to delve deeper into the specific challenges individuals face. This foundation enables us to approach each struggle with an open heart and mind, recognizing that every person's journey is unique and worthy of respect.

Furthermore, this understanding encourages us to cultivate empathy and compassion. When we recognize the diverse ways in which struggle manifests, we become less quick to judge and more inclined to offer support. We learn to listen with patience and understanding, providing a safe space for others to share their burdens and find solace.

In the chapters that follow, we will build upon this foundation, exploring practical strategies and spiritual insights to navigate the complexities of struggle. We will learn how to harness our strengths, embrace our vulnerabilities, and find meaning and purpose in our hardships. Together, we will journey through the diverse landscape of human struggle, discovering the resilience and hope that lies within each of us.

As we embark on this journey, let us remember the words of Psalm 46:1: *"God is our refuge and strength, an ever-present help in trouble."*

With this assurance, we can face our struggles with courage and faith, knowing that we are not alone and that every challenge is an opportunity for growth and transformation.

CHAPTER TWO

HOPE IN THE STRUGGLE

"Not only so, but we also glory in our sufferings, because we know that suffering produces perseverance; perseverance, character; and character, hope. And hope does not put us to shame, because God's love has been poured out into our hearts through the Holy Spirit, who has been given to us."

–Romans 5:3-4

Life is filled with trials that can often leave us feeling overwhelmed and hopeless. However, it is precisely in these moments of adversity that we can discover a profound and enduring sense of hope. This chapter explores the concept of hope amidst adversity, drawing on Christian teachings and personal stories to illustrate how hope can be found and sustained in the midst of life's challenges.

Hope is not merely wishful thinking or blind optimism; it is a deep-seated assurance that, despite the difficulties we face, there is a greater purpose and plan at work. In the Christian faith, hope is anchored in the promises of God and the belief that He is sovereign over all circumstances. Romans 8:28 reminds us, *"And we know that in all things God works for the good of those who love him, who have been called according to his purpose."*

The Bible is replete with stories of individuals who faced tremendous adversity yet found hope through their faith in God. Consider the story of Joseph, who was sold into slavery by his brothers, falsely accused, and imprisoned. Despite these hardships, Joseph remained faithful and eventually rose to a position of great influence in Egypt, saving many lives during a severe famine. His story is a powerful testament to the fact that God can bring good out of even the most dire situations (Genesis 37-50).

Another example is the Apostle Paul, who endured numerous hardships, including imprisonment, beatings, and shipwrecks. In his letter to the Philippians, Paul writes, *"I can do all this through him who gives me strength"* (Philippians 4:13). Paul's unwavering hope in God's provision and strength enabled him to persevere through his trials and continue spreading the message of Christ.

In our own lives, we can find hope by reflecting on the ways God has been faithful in the past and trusting in His promises for the future. Personal testimonies of overcoming adversity can serve as powerful reminders of God's presence and provision. Sharing these stories within a community of believers can also provide encouragement and support.

Consider the story of a woman who, after losing her job and facing financial instability, turned to her faith for strength. Through prayer and trust in God's plan, she found new opportunities and a renewed sense of purpose. Her story is a reminder that even in the darkest times, God is at work, providing hope and direction.

To cultivate hope, we can start with regular prayer and meditation on Scripture, which reinforces our belief in God's promises. Psalm 46:10 encourages us to *"Be still, and know that I am God."* Surrounding ourselves with a supportive community of believers can also provide encouragement and remind us that we are not alone in our struggles. Hebrews 10:24-25 urges us to *"spur one another on toward love and good deeds, not giving up meeting together...but encouraging one another."*

Keeping a gratitude journal and reflecting on past experiences of God's faithfulness can help us maintain a hopeful perspective. 1 Thessalonians 5:18 reminds us to *"give thanks in all circumstances; for this is God's will for you in Christ Jesus."* Serving others in need can shift our focus from our own struggles and remind us of the hope we have in Christ. Acts of service can also be a tangible expression of God's love and hope to others.

Hope in the struggle is not only possible but essential for navigating life's challenges. By grounding our hope in the promises of God and the truths of Scripture, we can find strength and resilience to persevere. As we trust in God's plan and seek His presence, we discover that hope is not just a fleeting feeling but a steadfast anchor for our souls. In the words of Hebrews 6:19, *"We have this hope as an anchor for the soul, firm and secure."*

Reflect on how you have experienced hope in the midst of personal struggles. What Scriptures or stories from the Bible have provided you with hope during difficult times? How can you cultivate a deeper sense of hope in your daily life?

Heavenly Father, thank You for the hope that we have in You. Help us to trust in Your promises and to find strength in Your presence, especially during times of adversity. Remind us of Your faithfulness and guide us to be sources of hope and encouragement to others. In Jesus' name, Amen.

Have you ever woken up one day to find yourself at the bottom of a pit, bewildered and lost, without any warning signs? That's exactly what happened to me. It felt like despair had struck overnight, leaving me exhausted and in a place, I could only hope to escape from once again. If you've been there, you know the constant battle it takes to break free.

In that dark pit, I noticed it was a cylinder about six feet in circumference, with walls made of dark, slippery mud. The mud streamed down, making the climb out seem impossible. As I glanced upward, searching for any sign of light, I saw a dim flicker in the distance, far away and almost unreachable. The weight of pain and uncertainty was heavy on my heart, and I questioned if I would survive this ordeal.

Early that morning, Lisa, who saw something was wrong, asked if I was okay. I assured her I was fine, though deep down, I was struggling. I believed that God's love was giving me the will to survive. My only hope was in my Redeemer, trusting that I would emerge from this dark and lonely place. His name holds power and can break any stronghold.

For the past two and a half years, I've been equipped with tools to face such darkness, but this pit was different. Lisa continued to check on me hour by hour, her concern both a comfort and a frustration. She understood where I was and tried to rescue me with her special way of throwing lifelines. But in the darkness, I couldn't see them.

If you've ever experienced a similar place of despair, you know the pain. Yet, even in that pit, I was not alone. There was another presence with me in the darkness. As the hours passed, it felt like I was living a dual life—a life of despair and a life of hope. Grabbing the lifeline of hope and speaking the name of Jesus, I began to climb out of the pit, slowly but surely.

That day, the darkness did not prevail. Lisa asked me one last time if I was okay, and my answer was simple, *"I am."* I shared with her the intense battle I had faced within myself in a pit deeper than any I had ever known. She understood and revealed that she had been praying for me to break every stronghold and emerge victorious. And I did, not by my own strength, but by the power of Jesus.

Invaluable tools given to me by a remarkable person helped me navigate the exhaustion, stress, and pain of life. This person understands human emotions like no one else, and with her guidance, coupled with my faith, everything falls into place. It's a delicate balance between faith and human emotions. Lisa, my sweet and wonderful lifeline, recognized the pit I was in, prayed for me, and encouraged me through my darkest hours.

Emerging from the pit is never easy. It's far simpler to fall into it, given our human nature. Our thoughts, emotions, and spirits must be constantly guarded. Keep looking up; that's where you will find hope, and His grace will restore all the broken pieces. Remember, you are never alone in your darkest moments. Hope is always within reach, even when it feels distant and dim. Trust in His power, lean on those who love you and believe that you can emerge victorious, just as I did.

2 Samuel 18:30 (ESV): *"And the king said, 'Turn aside and stand here.' So he turned aside and stood still."*

In memory of my brother, Chris, who died at the young age of thirty-seven, I write this story. It's been almost three years since he passed away. He ran as far as he could and as long as he could. His pain and suffering never left him. Finally, it took his life.

Chris and I had many memories on this pier, sitting there in the night hours with a dim light in the background, just enough to light up our faces. The sounds of the water were so calm, and to this day, I still hear the silence. Our conversations were always light and never too deep. Home would come up now and then, but we mostly talked about the future. Chris talked about his hopes and dreams, and I talked about mine.

Today, I visited the pier again, thinking of him and recalling the beautiful memories we had there. I usually stand right where he stood, look out over the water, and listen as if to hear his voice, but there is nothing but silence now. This is truly a special place, not just because this is where my brother once stood. This is also where my girls have stood, where many of my friends have stood, and where the love of my life now stands—my sweet Lisa. I love you, Lisa!

As Lisa and I sat there today, I carved our initials into the wood once again. I often do this because I forget where I have carved our initials in the past. There are hundreds of names carved on this pier. This tells me of all the others who have once stood here. Not just Boys Home boys and girls, but many in the community and many who came to vacation at Lake Waccamaw. Many dreams of love and a future were born here; the carvings tell me so.

Today, I was reminded by an old and new friend of just how short life can be. I called my friend for the first time in some thirty years. Her voice sounded the same as it did thirty years ago when she said, *"We can't meet today; someone has died, and we will be going to the funeral home."* As I listened to her explain, I felt sadness, not for missing our meeting, but for all of those who once had hopes and dreams like Chris. I was sad for those who loved her, and I knew what pain and suffering they were going through. As I walked out to the end of that pier today and stood where my brother once stood, I was reminded that life is brief and takes us places we never thought we would go. My journey has been filled with adventures, great joy, and many heartaches; I know I am blessed to still be standing where my brother once stood.

Life's journey is filled with twists and turns, many of which are unexplainable. For me, it is where my brother once stood. The memories I have will be part of me until I no longer stand. Then others will walk the same path as I have, stand where I stood, and say, *"I once stood here."* The water will whisper the hopes and dreams they had and will tell stories of the many who have stood there. We serve a wonderful God who has allowed me into so many lives, both the standing and the once-stood. I am thankful to each of you for sharing your lives with me, not just your hopes and dreams but also what has crushed you, caused you pain and suffering, turned your dreams into nightmares, and cursed you for a lifetime.

To end this story is impossible as life continues. To apply this story to your life and mine, we must stand where our brothers and sisters once stood. Lean on their memories, their hopes, and their dreams. Remember all the good in life and how blessed we are to still be where they once stood. I love you, Chris; thank you for the memories, the hopes, and the dreams of where you once stood.

Never let go of your hopes and dreams. This is where you stand today.

Reflecting on my brother Chris, who passed away at just thirty-seven, I remember his vibrant spirit and the dreams he shared with me on this very pier. Today, standing where he once stood, the memories flood back, reminding me of the fleeting nature of life and the hope we cling to even in the face of loss.

In moments like these, it can be challenging to find hope in God. Our circumstances may seem overwhelming, our paths unclear, and our hearts heavy with grief. Yet, as believers, we are reminded in Romans 5:3-5 that tribulations produce perseverance, proven character, and ultimately, hope that does not disappoint. This hope is grounded in the love of God, poured into our hearts through the Holy Spirit, as Jeremiah 29:11 assures us of God's plans to prosper us and give us hope and a future.

Psalm 42:5 echoes the struggle of despairing souls, urging us to find our hope in God, who promises to provide and sustain us through every trial. The journey of faith acknowledges that life's twists and turns are part of a larger plan—God's plan—which includes restoration, renewal, and the hope of eternal life (Titus 1:2; 1 Peter 1:13).

In exploring different types of hope, we recognize that worldly hope, devoid of faith, is fleeting and uncertain. True hope, rooted in faith in Jesus Christ, offers a deeper, lasting assurance of salvation and victory over adversity. As believers, this hope is not just an abstract concept but a living reality that sustains us through life's storms.

Drawing from theories on hope, such as Snyder's framework of goal orientation and agency thinking, we understand that hope is not passive but active—a force that motivates us to persevere and seek pathways to our desired goals. In social work and community contexts, hope becomes a powerful tool for healing and transformation, fostering resilience and optimism (Clark, 2012; Duncan-Andrade, 2009; Ginwright, 2015).

Practically, maintaining hope involves leaning on trusted friends, engaging with scripture for spiritual nourishment, and earnest prayer for guidance and strength. For those without faith, navigating life's challenges relies on philosophical approaches to resilience and coping mechanisms tailored to individual needs and beliefs.

As we navigate the complexities of life, whether through personal loss, societal challenges, or existential crises, let us hold fast to the hope that transcends circumstances. This hope, rooted in faith and sustained by God's promises, is a beacon of light in our darkest moments. May it empower us to face each day with courage, knowing that in Christ, we find true peace, joy, and hope that endures.

CHAPTER THREE

STRUGGLE WITH THE CHURCH

"Carry each other's burdens, and in this way you will fulfill the law of Christ."

– Galatians 6:2

Religious institutions, particularly the church, have long been viewed as pillars of support during times of struggle. Historically, churches have provided a sanctuary for the weary, a community for the lonely, and a source of guidance for the lost. However, as society evolves, the role of the church and its ability to support individuals through personal and communal struggles have come under scrutiny.

The traditional role of the church has always been multifaceted. Beyond being a place of worship, it has served as a center for community support and social services. Churches have organized food banks, shelters, and counseling services, addressing both the physical and emotional needs of their congregants. They have played pivotal roles in social movements, advocating for justice and equality. For many, the church has been a beacon of hope, a place where they could find solace and a sense of belonging.

However, modern-day challenges have shifted the landscape of religious support. Societal changes, including increased secularization and a decline in church attendance, have affected the church's ability to engage with and support individuals effectively. Many people feel a disconnect between the teachings of the church and the realities of their daily lives. The traditional messages and methods of the church sometimes seem out of touch with contemporary issues, leading to a sense of alienation among congregants.

One significant issue is the perceived rigidity of church doctrines. In a world that is increasingly embracing diversity and inclusivity, some church teachings are viewed as exclusionary. Issues such as LGBTQ+ rights, gender equality, and racial justice have highlighted the gap between modern societal values and traditional church doctrines. This has caused many to question the relevance of the church in their lives, feeling unsupported or even judged by an institution that once provided comfort.

Moreover, the leadership within many churches has come under fire for various reasons, including scandals and misuse of power. These incidents have eroded trust and led to disillusionment among congregants. When leaders fail to exemplify the values they preach, it creates a crisis of faith, not just in the religious aspect, but also in the institution itself.

Despite these challenges, there are still many examples of churches rising to the occasion and providing critical support. Some churches have adapted to the changing times by modernizing their approaches and becoming more inclusive. They have embraced technology to reach wider audiences, offered more relevant programming, and engaged in community activism that aligns with contemporary values.

Real-life stories illustrate the positive impact of such churches. For instance, in times of natural disasters, churches often mobilize quickly, providing essential services and emotional support to affected communities. During the COVID-19 pandemic, many churches transitioned to virtual services and found new ways to connect with and support their congregants, demonstrating resilience and adaptability.

However, the question remains: Are these efforts enough to bridge the gap between the church and those it aims to support? For many, the struggle with the church is not just about the institution's ability to provide support, but also about its willingness to evolve and meet people where they are. The challenge lies in balancing tradition with progress, and maintaining core values while also embracing change.

Ultimately, the relationship between individuals and the church is deeply personal and varies widely. Some find profound comfort and support within their religious communities, while others continue to struggle with feelings of alienation and disconnection. The future of the church's role in supporting individuals through struggles will depend on its ability to listen, adapt, and genuinely engage with the diverse needs of its congregants.

The biblical definition of the church is rich with meaning and deep significance. According to Scripture, the church is not merely a building or a physical location but is fundamentally the body of Christ. This is revealed in passages such as Colossians 1:14, 18; Ephesians 1:22–23; 4:12, 15–16; Romans 12:5; and 1 Corinthians 6:15; 12:12–27. Therefore, a local church comprises all the true New Covenant believers in that locality, embodying the spiritual and communal essence of what it means to be the church.

The word translated as "church" in the English Bible is "ekklesia," a Greek term combining "kaleo" (to call) with the prefix "ek" (out). Thus, "ekklesia" literally means "the called-out ones." This term emphasizes the nature of the church as a gathering or assembly of people who are called out for a specific purpose. In its original context, "ekklesia" was used to refer to a group of people summoned for a meeting, often with a common purpose or mission.

However, the English word "church" does not come from "ekklesia" but from the word "kuriakon," which means "dedicated to the Lord." This term was commonly used to refer to a holy place or temple. By the time Jerome translated the New Testament from Greek to Latin, it had become customary to use a derivative of "kuriakon" to translate "ekklesia." Consequently, the word "church" in English implies a sacred building or temple, which can be seen as a poor translation of "ekklesia" since it focuses on the physical structure rather than the assembly of believers.

A more accurate translation of "ekklesia" would be "assembly" because it highlights the idea of a gathering of people. This term is also synonymous with "synagogue," which means "to come together" or "a gathering." The focus is on the community of believers coming together for worship, fellowship, and mutual support.

The concept of the "Body of Christ" is central to understanding the church. Believers are united with Christ through spiritual baptism, and they are collectively referred to as the body of Christ (Romans 12:4-5; 1 Corinthians 12:11, 13, 18, 27; Colossians 1:18; Ephesians 5:30). This metaphor illustrates the idea that Christians around the world constitute the physical representation of Christ on earth. It emphasizes the interdependence of church members, each contributing uniquely to the whole while being diverse in their gifts and roles (Romans 12:4; 1 Corinthians 12:14-17).

In essence, the church is not confined to a building or a location but is defined by the people who comprise it. It is the community of believers, called out and united in their faith in Christ, who collectively embody His presence and work in the world. This understanding challenges us to see the church not just as a place we go to but as a living, dynamic body of people dedicated to following Christ and serving others.

The purpose of the church, as outlined in Scripture, is both profound and multifaceted. The Bible presents a clear vision of what the church is meant to be and do, providing a framework that contrasts sharply with some modern interpretations of church life.

Biblical Purpose of the Church

1. Great Commission: Making Disciples

- Matthew 28:19-20 (ESV): *"Go therefore and make disciples of all nations, baptizing them in the name of the Father and of the Son and of the Holy Spirit, teaching them to observe all that I have commanded you. And behold, I am with you always, to the end of the age."*

- This passage emphasizes the church's primary mission: to spread the gospel and make disciples of all nations. The Great Commission outlines the church's role in evangelism and teaching, reinforcing the idea that its purpose extends beyond the local congregation to a global mission.

2. Teaching and Community

- Colossians 3:16 (ESV): *"Let the word of Christ dwell in you richly, teaching and admonishing one another in all wisdom, singing psalms and hymns and spiritual songs, with thankfulness in your hearts to God."*

- Acts 2:42 (ESV): *"And they devoted themselves to the apostles' teaching and the fellowship, to the breaking of bread and the prayers."*

- The church is called to be a community where believers teach one another, engage in worship, and build each other up in faith. This communal aspect is crucial for spiritual growth and mutual encouragement.

3. Identity and Unity in Christ

- 1 Peter 2:9-10 (ESV): *"But you are a chosen race, a royal priesthood, a holy nation, a people for his own possession, that you may proclaim the excellencies of him who called you out of darkness into his marvelous light. Once you were not a people, but now you are God's people; once you had not received mercy, but now you have received mercy."*

- Ephesians 2:19-22 (ESV): *"So then you are no longer strangers and aliens, but you are fellow citizens with the saints and members of the household of God, built on the foundation of the apostles and prophets, Christ Jesus himself being the cornerstone, in whom the whole structure, being joined together, grows into a holy temple in the Lord. In him you also are being built together into a dwelling place for God by the Spirit."*

- The church is depicted as a unified body of believers, both individually and corporately identified with Christ. It functions as a spiritual household and a holy temple, symbolizing the unity and identity of believers as God's people.

4. Encouragement and Support

- 1 Thessalonians 5:11 (ESV): *"Therefore encourage one another and build one another up, just as you are doing."*

- Hebrews 10:25 (ESV): *"Not neglecting to meet together, as is the habit of some, but encouraging one another, and all the more as you see the Day drawing near."*

- The church is intended to be a place of mutual encouragement and support. Regular gatherings and fellowship are essential for building up believers and maintaining a sense of community.

5. Demonstrating God's Wisdom and Compassion

- Ephesians 3:10 (ESV): *"So that through the church the manifold wisdom of God might now be made known to the rulers and authorities in the heavenly places."*

- James 5:14 (ESV): *"Is anyone among you sick? Let him call for the elders of the church, and let them pray over him, anointing him with oil in the name of the Lord."*

- The church is called to manifest God's wisdom and compassion, providing both spiritual and practical support to its members. This includes prayer, healing, and demonstrating God's love through action.

6. Endurance and Resilience

- Matthew 16:18 (ESV): *"And I tell you, you are Peter, and on this rock I will build my church, and the gates of hell shall not prevail against it."*

- This passage underscores the church's resilience and its enduring role in the face of adversity. Despite challenges, the church is established by Christ and will persevere.

In recent decades, there has been a noticeable shift in how churches are perceived and how they operate. The rise of mega-churches, with their focus on motivational messages and expansive entertainment, contrasts sharply with the biblical vision of the church. This shift has led some to question whether modern churches fulfill their intended purpose as outlined in Scripture.

Many modern churches have embraced a business model, prioritizing self-sustenance and growth over traditional spiritual and communal roles. For some, this has resulted in a disconnect between the church's activities and its biblical mandate. The emphasis on motivational speaking and entertainment can sometimes overshadow the church's core mission of discipleship, teaching, and community support.

Reflecting on this shift, it is evident that while some churches have adapted to contemporary culture, others may have drifted away from their foundational purpose. For those seeking a church experience aligned with biblical principles, smaller community churches may offer a more authentic representation of the church's role as envisioned in Scripture. These churches often emphasize direct involvement in God's work, community service, and a focus on teaching and fellowship.

It is important to recognize that this observation is not a critique of the church as a whole but rather a reflection on the evolving landscape of church life. The challenge for the modern church is to balance contemporary methods with timeless principles, ensuring that it remains true to its scriptural purpose while effectively engaging with today's world.

Over the past 35 years, my perception of the role of the church in supporting individuals during personal crises has evolved significantly. Reflecting on my experiences, there was a time when churches were swift to respond to needs within the community, regardless of whether the individuals in need were members or not. The church, in those days, transcended boundaries and came together to assist anyone in distress. This collective action was not driven by self-interest but by a genuine desire to serve and support.

However, as time has progressed, I've observed a gradual but noticeable shift. Modern-day churches, particularly those with a more self-serving approach, seem to focus more on their public image and community status rather than on direct, tangible support. This shift has occurred incrementally, and it's important to acknowledge that not all churches have followed this trend. Many small, community-focused churches continue to make a significant impact, influencing their local cultures in meaningful ways and serving those in need with dedication and compassion.

In contrast, some contemporary churches appear to be more concerned with aligning their activities with what is culturally acceptable or beneficial to their own interests. This shift has led to a focus on gaining exposure and visibility, sometimes at the expense of genuine community service. I've encountered pastors who view community involvement primarily as a means of enhancing the church's public relations, which raises concerns about the authenticity of their commitment to serving others.

The discrepancy between the biblical definition of the church and the reality of many modern-day churches is striking. The Bible defines the church as the "body of Christ," a collective of believers united in faith and mission, with a purpose to spread the gospel, support one another, and serve the broader community (Matthew 28:19-20; Colossians 3:16; 1 Peter 2:9-10; Ephesians 2:19-22). This vision includes being a beacon of hope and support for all, transcending self-interest and cultural trends.

In contrast, some modern churches may prioritize self-preservation and social status over these foundational purposes. The challenge is to align contemporary church practices with the biblical model, ensuring that the church remains a true reflection of Christ's mission and a genuine force for good in the community. It's crucial for churches to evaluate their role not just in terms of visibility or influence but in terms of their commitment to serving others and fulfilling their spiritual and communal responsibilities as defined by Scripture.

Everyone encounters struggles in life—whether related to health, addiction, financial difficulties, or family issues. During such times, the church has the potential to play a pivotal role in providing support and demonstrating compassion. A profound example of this is the experience of my brother, Chris.

Chris struggled with drug addiction and had little interest in the church, largely due to a perceived sense of judgment. However, after completing rehab, he decided to visit a local church. This decision marked a turning point in his life. The church he encountered was led by a godly man who had a deep understanding of addiction and recovery. This church did not judge Chris; instead, it embraced him with understanding and support. It became a place where he found faith and hope, leading him to accept Jesus as his savior. This transformation was both profound and beautiful.

The support Chris received extended beyond his personal struggle. My wife, Lisa, and I, who were initially uninterested in church, were invited by Chris to join him. Eventually, we, too, became believers. Despite Chris's ongoing battle with addiction, the church remained a steadfast support system for him. They provided not only spiritual guidance but also practical help when needed.

Even when Chris faced setbacks and was in and out of the church, its commitment to him never wavered. Sadly, his struggle ultimately claimed his life, but the impact of that church remained significant. Chris carried his Bible with him until the end, a symbol of the transformative support he received.

This experience illustrates what the church can be at its best: a place of acceptance, support, and unwavering commitment, making a genuine difference in the lives of those it serves.

Local, small community churches often exemplify adaptability in meeting the evolving needs of their members during challenging times. These churches continue to address issues such as sickness, financial burdens, and other personal struggles with compassion and practical support. They have evolved with the times while staying true to their scriptural foundation and community role.

In contrast, some modern-day churches—particularly those that originated from smaller congregations—seem to have lost touch with their foundational purpose. The shift from humble beginnings to large, self-serving institutions has led to practices that can feel detached from the core mission of the church.

For instance, some pastors of these modern churches live in opulent homes and may exhibit a disconnect from community issues like homelessness. When faced with requests for assistance, their responses can be dismissive, often suggesting that individuals simply "get a job" without addressing underlying issues.

Moreover, modern churches sometimes impose bureaucratic hurdles on those seeking help. Instead of offering immediate assistance, individuals may need to navigate a complex process, including filling out paperwork and attending meetings to determine if their need is deemed "worthy." This approach can feel more like a financial institution than a supportive community.

In contrast, small community churches often maintain a more straightforward approach. If someone is in need, they provide help without judgment or excessive requirements. This simplicity and directness align more closely with the church's role as a compassionate and supportive presence in the community.

The evolution of the church's role in addressing member needs highlights a significant shift in focus. While some churches continue to faithfully serve their communities, others have strayed from their foundational mission, prioritizing self-interest and institutional goals over direct, compassionate support. This disparity underscores the importance of aligning church practices with the biblical vision of service and community engagement.

The balance between spiritual guidance and practical support is crucial for churches as they navigate crises. Spiritual guidance and practical support are not mutually exclusive; rather, they should complement each other to provide holistic care for individuals in need.

Spiritual guidance is foundational, offering hope, comfort, and a sense of purpose through prayer and faith. It can provide strength and perspective, helping individuals navigate their challenges with a deeper understanding of their spiritual journey. However, while spiritual guidance is essential, it must be balanced with practical support. This balance means recognizing that while faith is a powerful tool, action, and practical steps are also necessary to address immediate needs.

A purely spiritual approach—such as simply praying and waiting for divine intervention—can sometimes overlook the practical actions required to address pressing issues. For example, someone facing financial hardship or a health crisis needs not only prayer but also tangible support, such as financial assistance or medical treatment. The idea is to "pray as if it depends on God and work as if it depends on you," ensuring that both spiritual and practical needs are addressed.

An example of the imbalance between spiritual and practical support is illustrated by the story of a woman with stage 4 cancer who was prayed for and told she was healed. She chose to forgo medical treatment based on this assurance. Tragically, she later died from her illness. This situation raises important questions about the role of spiritual guidance in the context of practical needs. While faith and prayer are vital, they should not replace medical advice or necessary actions.

In this case, the church's spiritual guidance provided hope, but it lacked the practical support needed for a well-rounded approach to the woman's situation. The balance would have been more effective if the church had offered both spiritual support and practical assistance, such as encouraging her to pursue medical treatments while continuing to provide spiritual comfort.

Effective management of this balance involves acknowledging that faith and action should work together. Churches should provide spiritual encouragement while also addressing practical needs through support services, community resources, and direct assistance. This approach ensures that individuals receive comprehensive care that respects their spiritual beliefs and meets their immediate needs.

The ideal balance between spiritual guidance and practical support involves integrating both aspects to provide a well-rounded approach to crisis management. By doing so, churches can better serve their communities and support individuals through their challenges in a meaningful and effective manner.

Within many church communities, there is often a stark contrast in how moral and personal struggles are addressed. Some churches maintain a rigid stance, suggesting that individuals with moral challenges should seek help elsewhere or even leave the church. This can be particularly harsh when someone is grappling with personal failings, such as sin. The sentiment might be: *"You are a sinner, and we can't have that here."*

Conversely, there are churches—though increasingly rare—that advocate for a more compassionate approach. These congregations may encourage individuals to repent and openly confess their sins, allowing for a process of restoration within the church community. A notable example from a decade ago illustrates this approach. A member of our congregation admitted to committing adultery. Despite the initial judgment, he was supported in confessing his sins publicly, alongside his wife. This act of repentance led to his restoration, and the church rallied around his family with love and support. This process, while complex, ended the rumor mill and contributed to the family's healing and continued joy. Although the effects of his past actions lingered, the church's support facilitated a powerful and redemptive journey.

Faith plays a pivotal role in my personal approach to overcoming challenges. I firmly believe in the entirety of the Bible, seeing it as a guide for all aspects of life. This belief is rooted in the faith that God has graciously given me through His Holy Spirit since 1988. My faith is centered around the Word of God, and I strive to live according to its teachings.

Life's struggles, such as when my wife, Lisa, was diagnosed with cancer, test our faith in profound ways. During such times, our faith provided strength and reassurance, guiding us through emotional turmoil and ultimately leading to a positive outcome. Hebrews 11:1 speaks to this confidence in hope and assurance in the unseen, while Ephesians 3:16-17 emphasizes the spiritual strength provided through faith.

Faith transforms struggle into opportunities for deeper understanding and growth. It doesn't eliminate worry or tribulations, but it instills a profound assurance that everything will be okay, making even the hardest times bearable and meaningful.

Religious leaders and institutions often face challenges when offering support during crises. Too frequently, I have observed leaders providing inadequate or misguided counsel, such as dismissing concerns with platitudes or offering superficial advice. This approach can be damaging, as it lacks the depth and compassion required for effective support.

In contrast, a well-trained biblical counselor or a resourceful support system can offer balanced, empathetic guidance that aligns with both scripture and practical wisdom. My own experience highlights the importance of seeking counsel from trusted individuals. In a recent struggle, I chose to consult a close friend who happened to be a therapist rather than a church leader or biblical counselor. Her support, which was both professional and compassionate, helped me navigate my difficulties without judgment.

Religious leaders have an ethical responsibility to offer support that is both loving and grounded in biblical principles. They should also be prepared to provide or direct individuals to resources that offer comprehensive help. By doing so, churches can enhance their role in supporting their members through struggles, ultimately strengthening the community and bringing glory to God.

While the church's approach to supporting members in crisis can vary widely, those who offer genuine, faith-based support can help transform struggles into opportunities for growth and restoration. The ethical responsibility of religious leaders is to provide balanced, compassionate counsel and to ensure that their congregation has access to appropriate resources.

CHAPTER FOUR
TRANSPARENCY HAS ITS STRUGGLE

"Anxiety in a man's heart weighs him down, but a good word makes him glad."

–Proverbs 12:25

In a world where images are curated carefully and every post on social media is a snapshot of the best moments, transparency stands out as a rare and often challenging virtue. When it comes to sharing personal narratives and struggles, transparency is not just about honesty; it is about being real, no matter the reality of what others might think about us. It requires a level of courage and vulnerability that can be both transformative and isolating.

Transparency, as I define it, is one of the most important values in our modern age. It goes beyond merely telling the truth; it involves opening up about the raw, unfiltered aspects of our lives—the parts we usually hide or gloss over to maintain a certain image. In a society where we often prioritize pleasing others and fitting in over staying true to our values, being transparent can feel like swimming against the current. It means embracing our struggles, flaws, and failures, and sharing them openly, regardless of how they might be perceived.

One of the most significant examples of transparency in my own life occurred while I was teaching a Sunday school class for young adults. During one session, I felt compelled to share some of my past experiences—specifically, the troubles I faced as a youth. I wanted to connect with my students on a deeper level and show them that it's okay to have a difficult past and still strive for better. I hoped my story would inspire them to be open about their own struggles and to understand that they are not alone.

However, my transparency was met with backlash. Parents of the students, along with the church leadership, expressed their concerns about the potential negative impact my story could have on the young adults and the church community as a whole. They believed that revealing such personal details might undermine my authority and influence as a teacher. I was advised to tone down my transparency to avoid causing any discomfort or controversy.

This experience highlighted the complex nature of transparency. On one hand, being open and honest can foster genuine connections and provide comfort to those who are struggling. On the other hand, it can also make us vulnerable to criticism and judgment. The struggle of transparency lies in balancing the need to be authentic with the potential repercussions of exposing our true selves.

Despite the challenges, I believe that transparency is crucial for personal growth and building meaningful relationships. When we share our struggles and vulnerabilities, we create a space where others feel safe to do the same. It breaks down the walls of isolation and fosters a sense of community and understanding. While it may not always be easy or well-received, the benefits of transparency far outweigh the costs.

In reflecting on my own journey, I realize that transparency has its struggle, but it also has its strength. It allows us to be true to ourselves and to connect with others on a deeper level. It reminds us that we are all imperfect and that our struggles are a natural part of the human experience. By embracing transparency, we can create a more compassionate and authentic world, one story at a time.

The tension between openness and vulnerability is a delicate balance. While both involve sharing aspects of ourselves with others, the depth and impact of these actions differ significantly. Openness is the willingness to share information, to be honest and straightforward, but often within comfortable limits. Vulnerability, on the other hand, involves exposing deeper, more sensitive parts of ourselves, risking judgment, and emotional pain in the process.

Being open can be seen as a controlled act of sharing. It is a choice to let others in, but only to a certain extent. Openness allows us to share our stories, thoughts, and feelings without necessarily diving into the rawest, most painful details. It's like opening a door just enough for someone to see inside but not wide enough for them to step through and explore every corner.

Vulnerability is the act of laying ourselves bare, with no control over how our shared truths will be received or judged. It's akin to laying down on the tracks, waiting for the train of emotions and judgment to pass over us, and allowing ourselves to fully experience whatever comes our way. Vulnerability involves the risk of being hurt but also holds the potential for profound connection and healing.

In my own life, I have encountered numerous situations where the tension between openness and vulnerability became evident. When I shared my troubled past with the Sunday school class, I was practicing vulnerability. I wasn't just being open about my experiences; I was exposing myself to potential criticism and backlash. The reactions I received demonstrated the risks associated with vulnerability. While some may have felt inspired or understood, others felt uncomfortable or even threatened by my honesty.

Discernment plays a critical role in deciding when to be transparent and how much to share. There are times when maintaining privacy is necessary, not out of a desire to hide the truth but to protect oneself and others from unnecessary harm or misunderstanding. For example, sharing deeply personal struggles with someone who is not equipped to respond with empathy or support can lead to further hurt and isolation.

The Bible provides guidance on this balance. In Ephesians 4:25, Paul emphasizes the importance of honesty and openness in building a community of faith: *"Therefore each of you must put off falsehood and speak truthfully to your neighbor, for we are all members of one body."* This verse highlights the value of transparency in fostering genuine relationships and community.

However, the Bible also acknowledges the complexity of human interactions and the need for discernment. In Matthew 7:6, Jesus advises, *"Do not give dogs what is sacred; do not throw your pearls to pigs. If you do, they may trample them under their feet, and turn and tear you to pieces."* This metaphor illustrates the importance of knowing when and with whom to share our most precious and vulnerable parts.

Transparency is often linked with the idea of light in the biblical context—revealing, illuminating, and guiding. Jesus

Himself said, "*Let your light shine before others, that they may see your good deeds and glorify your Father in heaven*" (Matthew 5:16). This metaphor speaks to the power of transparency to reveal the truth, guide others, and reflect the character of God in our actions.

At the same time, the Bible addresses the challenges of being transparent in a world that often values appearances over authenticity. Jesus' admonition of the Pharisees in Matthew 23, where He calls for sincerity of heart rather than mere outward compliance, underscores the struggle between outward show and inner reality.

In the complexities of transparency, we must constantly evaluate our motivations and the potential impact of our openness. It is essential to be true to ourselves while also considering the well-being of those around us. Transparency, when approached with wisdom and discernment, can lead to deeper connections, healing, and a more authentic way of living.

Ultimately, the pursuit of transparency is a journey towards truth and authenticity. It is about shining our light, even when it feels vulnerable, and trusting that by doing so, we can create a more compassionate and understanding world. The struggle of transparency is real, but so are its rewards. By embracing this struggle, we can find strength in our vulnerability and discover the profound beauty of living authentically.

Determining when to trust someone with your personal story took me many years to navigate. I have written about this journey in my book *The Invisible Soul, Rise Up,* and on my blog, where I am most transparent. The fear of judgment was a significant barrier. I wanted to live a life free from judgment, but that wasn't possible. Some will judge you regardless of your story. You must craft your narrative carefully and share just enough to engage appropriately. Ephesians 4:15 says, *"Instead, speaking the truth in love, we will grow to become in every respect the mature body of him who is the head, that is, Christ."*

I have regretted sharing something personal with someone. The people you trust most can become adversaries without realizing it. I always advise keeping your circle small and allowing it to grow harmoniously and honestly. Reflecting on what is true and just is crucial, as Philippians 4:8 emphasizes: *"Finally, brothers, whatever is true, whatever is honorable, whatever is just, whatever is pure, whatever is lovely, whatever is commendable, if there is any excellence, if there is anything worthy of praise, think about these things."*

A notable real-life example of transparency leading to unexpected outcomes is from when I worked for a company that monitored its employees' social media content. I posted about one of my therapy sessions on my blog. The department head confronted me and instructed me to delete the post, fearing it could blemish the organization's values and mission. I refused and later sought new employment. This experience reminded me of 3 John 1:4: *"I have no greater joy than to hear that my children are walking in the truth."*

Being too open also has risks. Every transparent truth can face counter untruths that seek to undermine and destroy it. Followers of Christ are called to be honest within the body, as transparency allows for mutual encouragement and accountability. This practice is vital for spiritual growth but requires discernment regarding who truly follows Christ.

Effective strategies for balancing transparency and maintaining boundaries in relationships include understanding biblical transparency. Ephesians 5:8-9 reminds us that as followers of Jesus, we have moved from darkness to light. We must walk in this light and live truthfully as members of one another. James 5:16 instructs us to confess our sins to fellow believers. However, it is essential to set relationship boundaries and trust only those who have proven to be real with you. The absence of rumors and gossip in the congregation is a sign of healthy transparency.

Approaching transparency in different contexts involves humility in personal relationships, avoiding pride in conversations, and using wisdom and prayer in public platforms. For example, a group member's public disclosure of a struggle may not always be appropriate. Transparency should be approached cautiously, with trusted friends and family.

My experience with transparency has affected my relationships positively and negatively. Sharing struggles at a men's meeting can lead to judgment but also genuine support from those who care. Transparency does not seek approval from others but aims to bear one another's burdens, as Galatians 6:2 and Psalms teach. Community bonds strengthen when members support each other through struggles, as seen when group members rallied to support Tyler after his job loss.

Cultural and social norms significantly influence perspectives on transparency and openness. Social platforms often feature "posers" who offer advice without understanding the struggle. True transparency should be reserved for trusted spaces, not broadcasted on social platforms. Cultural sensitivity is also vital. For instance, inviting someone struggling with lust to a conservative setting rather than a triggering environment is more supportive.

For those considering being more transparent about personal struggles, I advise embracing vulnerability with courage, rooted in one's identity in Christ. Transparency builds mutual encouragement and sanctification. Living transparently is more about God's work than personal comfort. While it can be challenging, it strengthens relationships and communities.

Navigating the risks and rewards of sharing personal stories involves genuine trust and comfort in one's identity. As Nehemiah 2:2 shows, transparent behavior reflects true feelings. Trusting God and others allows us to be real and open, fostering acceptance and support. Romans 15:7 encourages us to accept one another as Christ accepted us, promoting transparent behavior. Making others feel safe to be themselves and sharing our struggles openly creates an environment of trust and support. Transparency can lead to deeper connections and mutual encouragement, reinforcing community bonds.

CHAPTER FIVE

JUDGMENT AND PEOPLE IN THE STRUGGLE

No matter what we think or say, judging and feeling judged is something deeply embedded in us all. The judgment of others is inevitable. It's human nature to judge; that's why the Bible warns us not to judge. We can observe and talk about it but not judge the individual who's going through some sort of struggle. The attitudes of close friends and family often wield the greatest influence when someone is facing a struggle. Regardless of the nature of the struggle, what is needed most is guidance and hope rather than judgment. The way others respond can significantly affect the trajectory of the person's journey through their difficulties, and, in severe cases, can even lead to fatal outcomes.

"Do not judge others, and you will not be judged. For you will be treated as you treat others. The standard you use in judging is the standard by which you will be judged. And why worry about a speck in your friend's eye when you have a log in your own? How can you think of saying to your friend, 'Let me help you get rid of that speck in your eye,' when you can't see past the log in your own eye? Hypocrite! First get rid of the log in your own eye; then you will see well enough to deal with the speck in your friend's eye."

— Matthew 7:1-5

Thankfully, as Christians, we have answers for this judgment. We deserve to be rightly condemned, and yet Jesus took both that condemnation and punishment for us on the cross. He substituted His righteousness for our faults.

In one sense, it's okay and even good to call sin for what it is and not mince words. Absolute truth and moral right and wrong are not subjective to what media, politicians, or social media say. But as fellow sinners, we have no place to judge humanity. We can leave that to a perfect God and pray for His grace and forgiveness over that person and us in the same way.

Judgment is a universal experience—one that is as natural as breathing. No matter how much we might try to avoid it, judgment from others is inevitable. It often comes from those closest to us: friends, family, colleagues, and even strangers. What makes judgment particularly impactful is not just its presence but the way it shapes our lives, especially during times of struggle.

When we are faced with difficulties, we look for solutions, guidance, and, most importantly, hope. Yet, all too often, we are met with judgment instead. This judgment can come in many forms—disapproving looks, harsh words, or even the silent withdrawal of support. It's a heavy burden to bear, especially when it comes from those we hold dear. Their judgment doesn't just add weight to our struggles; it can steer us off course entirely.

One of the most harmful effects of judgment is its ability to block the very answers we seek. In our most vulnerable moments, we are not only searching for solutions but also for validation, for a sense that we are not alone in our pain. Judgment isolates us, making us feel as though we are beyond help or hope. It silences the voices that could offer us support, replacing them with a chorus of criticism and condemnation.

Consider a person who is battling an addiction, dealing with a financial crisis, or struggling with a mental health issue. These are situations where the need for support and understanding is paramount. Yet, when judgment enters the picture, it has the power to push that person deeper into their struggle. Instead of feeling uplifted and encouraged, they may feel overwhelmed by shame, guilt, and despair. Judgment can make them question their worth, leading them to believe that they are undeserving of help or incapable of change.

This is where the real danger lies. Judgment not only compounds the struggle but also has the potential to drive a person to the brink of despair. In the darkest moments, when hope seems out of reach, judgment can be the force that pushes someone over the edge. It can lead to self-destructive behavior, isolation, and, in the worst cases, even death. The emotional and psychological toll of judgment is profound, and its effects can be devastating.

The emotional impact of judgment is something that cannot be overstated. When we are judged, especially by those closest to us, it affects us on a deep, personal level. It challenges our sense of self-worth and can lead to feelings of inadequacy, shame, and hopelessness.

In the midst of a struggle, these feelings can be amplified. The person who is already battling their own demons now has to contend with the added burden of judgment from others. This can lead to a vicious cycle where the struggle feeds the judgment, and the judgment feeds the struggle. It's a cycle that is difficult to break and one that can have long-lasting effects on a person's mental and emotional health.

Psychologically, judgment can lead to a range of negative outcomes, including anxiety, depression, and a deep sense of loneliness. The person who is judged may begin to internalize the negative opinions of others, leading them to believe that they are fundamentally flawed or unworthy of love and support. This can erode their confidence and self-esteem, making it even more difficult for them to overcome their struggles.

The emotional toll of judgment can also manifest in physical ways. Stress, sleeplessness, and other health issues can arise as a result of the constant pressure and negativity that judgment brings. The body and mind are connected, and when one is under attack, the other often suffers as well.

In the face of judgment, hope becomes a crucial lifeline. Hope is what gives us the strength to persevere, even when the odds seem insurmountable. It's the belief that things can get better, that there is a light at the end of the tunnel, no matter how faint it may seem.

But where does this hope come from? For many, it comes from faith—faith in God, in the goodness of humanity, and in the possibility of redemption. The Bible teaches us that judgment is not ours to give; that role belongs to God alone. As humans, we are flawed, and our judgments are often clouded by our own biases, fears, and insecurities. Instead of judging others, we are called to offer compassion, understanding, and support.

This is where true hope lies. It's found in the knowledge that we are not defined by the judgments of others but by the grace of God. It's the understanding that, despite our struggles, we are worthy of love, forgiveness, and redemption. Hope allows us to rise above the harsh words and critical glances, to continue our journey toward healing and growth.

When we replace judgment with hope, we not only help ourselves but also those around us. By choosing to offer support instead of criticism, we become a beacon of light for others who are struggling. We show them that they are not alone, that their struggles do not define them, and that there is always a path forward.

In order to overcome the harmful effects of judgment, we must actively work to build communities of support. These are spaces where people can share their struggles without fear of judgment, and where they can find the encouragement and guidance they need to move forward.

Creating such communities starts with each of us. It requires a commitment to empathy, compassion, and understanding. We must be willing to listen without judgment, to offer help without criticism, and to love without conditions. It's about being there for one another in the truest sense, offering a shoulder to lean on and a hand to hold.

In these communities, hope can flourish. People are empowered to face their struggles head-on, knowing that they have a support system behind them. They are reminded that they are not alone and that there is always a way forward, no matter how difficult the journey may be.

As we navigate our own struggles and the struggles of those around us, we are faced with a choice. We can choose to judge, criticize, and condemn, or we can choose to offer hope, support, and love. The choice we make has a profound impact not only on our own lives but also on the lives of others.

Judgment is easy. It's a reflex, a reaction that comes naturally to us as humans. But just because it's easy doesn't mean it's right. The harder, more rewarding path is the one that leads to understanding, compassion, and hope.

In choosing this path, we open the door to healing and growth. We create spaces where people feel safe to share their struggles, and where they can find the strength and courage to overcome even the most difficult challenges. And in doing so, we fulfill our calling as Christians—to love one another as Christ has loved us.

So, as you move forward in your own journey, remember the words of Matthew 7:1-5. Do not judge others, and you will not be judged. Instead, choose to offer hope, to build others up, and to walk alongside them in their struggles. For in the end, it is not judgment that will bring us closer to God, but the love and support we offer to one another in our times of need.

When we go through a struggle, whether it's personal, professional, or spiritual, one thing becomes painfully clear: the true nature of our friendships and social networks. The obvious truth is that the friends who stay with you, who remain steadfast and nonjudgmental, are the ones who truly care. They are the ones who understand that struggle is a part of life and that their role is to support, not to judge.

On the other hand, those who judge—whether they are Christian or not—will ultimately distance themselves, either at the onset of the struggle or in the thick of it. The abandonment of these so-called friends can be subtle or abrupt, but the impact is profound. They often claim they are "giving you space" or want you to "figure things out on your own." But this abandonment, whether deliberate or passive, adds another layer of complexity to an already difficult situation.

When the struggle passes, these friends may try to re-enter your life, perhaps under the guise of rekindling the old bond. However, these reunions are often short-lived. The memory of their absence during your time of need taints the relationship. What they see as "giving space" is often perceived as abandonment by the person who was left alone in their struggle. This perceived abandonment can lead to feelings of betrayal, making it difficult, if not impossible, to fully restore the friendship to what it once was.

Friends and social networks play a critical role in either supporting or hindering someone during a struggle. The initial response of your social circle when the struggle begins often sets the tone for what lies ahead. True friends will rally behind you, offering their time, energy, and resources to help you navigate through the storm. These are the people who provide emotional support, practical assistance, and a nonjudgmental ear. They may not have all the answers, but their willingness to stand by you speaks volumes.

However, not all friends will be so supportive. In some cases, the struggle may force your friends to choose sides, especially if the struggle involves conflict or controversy. This can lead to a split in your social network, where some people offer support while others distance themselves. The loss of social support can have a significant impact on the outcome of your struggle, either positively or negatively. A fractured social network can lead to feelings of isolation and despair, while a unified one can provide the strength and encouragement needed to overcome the challenges.

Relationships inevitably shift when someone is going through a difficult period. The dynamics change and the nature of these shifts often depends on how others perceive and react to the struggle. Judgment plays a significant role in these changes. When people judge, they tend to distance themselves. They may not want to be associated with the struggle or the person going through it, especially if they see it as a reflection of their own fears or insecurities.

The problem is that, more often than not, everyone is dealing with their own struggles. This makes it difficult for them to muster the energy or emotional bandwidth to support someone else. When faced with the struggles of others, people may say things like, "I don't know what to tell you," or "I just can't help you right now." These statements, while perhaps honest, reveal the underlying strain that judgment places on relationships. It's easier to judge than to expend the energy to help. It's easier to stand on the sidelines, offering commentary, than to jump into the fray and offer real support.

This strain can cause friendships and social connections to fray or even break. The person going through the struggle may feel abandoned, while those who judge may feel justified in their distance. The relationship, once a source of strength and comfort, becomes another battleground, adding to the emotional and psychological toll of the struggle.

Judgment, whether spoken or unspoken, is often the silent saboteur of relationships during difficult times. It creates a barrier between the person struggling and those around them. Instead of empathy, judgment fosters misunderstanding and alienation. It allows people to distance themselves, to rationalize their lack of support, and to maintain a sense of superiority or detachment.

For the person on the receiving end, judgment feels like a betrayal. It deepens the sense of isolation and can exacerbate the struggle, making it harder to find a way forward. Instead of feeling supported, they feel scrutinized and alone, as if their worth is being measured by their ability to overcome their difficulties without faltering.

In the end, judgment is easier than offering help, but it comes at a great cost. It not only damages relationships but also hinders the healing and recovery process. True support requires effort, understanding, and a willingness to stand by someone even when the road is rough. It means choosing compassion over criticism and connection over distance.

Struggles reveal the true nature of our relationships. They show us who our real friends are—the ones who stay, who support, who don't judge. They also expose the fragility of friendships built on convenience or superficiality. When judgment enters the picture, it can destroy even the strongest of bonds, leaving us to navigate our struggles alone.

But there is a silver lining. Struggles also offer an opportunity to strengthen our social networks, to build deeper, more meaningful connections with those who are willing to stand by us. By recognizing the role of judgment and its impact on our relationships, we can make more conscious choices about the people we surround ourselves with. We can choose to foster friendships that are based on mutual support and understanding, rather than those that crumble at the first sign of difficulty.

Judgment, in its various forms, is one of the most insidious barriers to personal growth and resilience. It can manifest through the disapproving looks of strangers, the harsh words of a loved one, or the internalized criticism we carry within ourselves. While it may seem like a natural part of social interaction, judgment can deeply hinder an individual's ability to grow, adapt, and recover from life's challenges.

Personal growth is often a journey that requires vulnerability, self-exploration, and the courage to face uncomfortable truths. When judgment enters the picture, it can create a hostile environment that stifles this process. Instead of feeling safe to explore and expand, individuals may become defensive, retreat into themselves, or conform to the expectations of others to avoid criticism. This fear of judgment can prevent people from taking risks, trying new things, or even acknowledging their own desires and needs.

For instance, consider the story of a young woman who found herself trapped in a toxic marriage. Her husband, a narcissist, constantly judged and criticized her, chipping away at her self-esteem and sense of identity. Over time, she became a shell of her former self, unable to see her worth or potential. Her personal growth was stunted because she was living under the constant scrutiny of someone who sought to mold her into his own ideal, rather than allowing her to flourish as her own person.

It was only through counseling that she began to reclaim her sense of self. With the help of a therapist, she recognized the damaging effects of her husband's judgment and started to rebuild her confidence. Remarkably, her husband eventually joined her in therapy, where he too learned the destructive nature of his behavior. This rare case of mutual growth highlights the power of overcoming judgment—but it also underscores how devastating judgment can be when left unchecked.

Resilience is the ability to bounce back from adversity, to endure hardship, and to keep moving forward despite setbacks. It is a quality that allows individuals to recover from life's most challenging moments. However, judgment can severely undermine this resilience. When people are judged, particularly during times of struggle, it can sap their strength and erode their will to persevere.

Judgment creates an environment where the person struggling feels even more isolated and misunderstood. Instead of receiving the support and encouragement needed to build resilience, they are met with criticism or indifference, which can lead to self-doubt and hopelessness. The energy that could be used to overcome challenges is instead spent trying to defend oneself, mitigate the impact of judgment, or internalize the negative perceptions of others.

The story of the young woman in a toxic marriage is just one example of how judgment can stifle personal development.

There are countless other instances where judgment has prevented individuals from reaching their full potential.

For example, consider a promising young athlete who, despite his talent, faces constant judgment from his coach for not fitting the traditional mold of what an athlete should be. Perhaps he's not as tall, not as muscular, or doesn't have the same demeanor as his peers. The coach's judgment, whether overt or subtle, creates an environment where the athlete feels inadequate and begins to doubt his abilities. Instead of focusing on improving his skills, he becomes consumed by the need to meet unrealistic standards, and his performance suffers as a result.

In another case, imagine an artist who is constantly judged by her family for pursuing a career in the arts instead of a more "practical" profession. Their judgment, masked as concern, instills a fear of failure in her. Every time she starts a new project, she hears their voices in her head, questioning her choices and predicting her downfall. This judgment paralyzes her creativity, making it difficult for her to fully express herself or take the necessary risks to grow as an artist.

These examples highlight how judgment can derail personal development by instilling fear, self-doubt, and a sense of inadequacy.

Judgment undermines resilience in several ways. Firstly, it erodes self-confidence. When someone is judged, especially by those they respect or care about, it can make them question their worth and capabilities. This erosion of self-confidence makes it harder to bounce back from setbacks because the individual begins to believe they are not capable of overcoming challenges.

Secondly, judgment creates a sense of isolation. When people feel judged, they often withdraw from others, fearing further criticism. This isolation deprives them of the social support that is crucial for building resilience. Without a network of supportive relationships, it becomes much more difficult to recover from adversity.

Lastly, judgment can lead to internalized negativity. When people are repeatedly judged, they may start to internalize the negative opinions of others, adopting them as their own beliefs. This internalized negativity becomes a self-fulfilling prophecy, where the individual begins to sabotage their own efforts, believing they are destined to fail.

For those who draw strength from their faith, the Bible offers numerous examples of resilience in the face of judgment and adversity. The stories of Paul and Job, in particular, demonstrate how resilience can be maintained even when facing severe trials and judgment from others.

Paul's resilience is evident throughout his missionary journey. Despite being beaten, stoned, and left for dead, Paul continued his mission undeterred. His resilience was rooted in his unwavering faith in God's plan, which allowed him to rise above the judgment and persecution he faced.

Similarly, Job's story is one of incredible resilience in the face of unimaginable suffering. Despite losing everything—his wealth, his children, and his health—Job refused to curse God or give in to despair. His resilience was born out of his deep faith and trust in God's sovereignty, even when his friends judged him and his wife urged him to give up.

These biblical examples highlight how resilience is not just about physical endurance but also about spiritual strength. For believers, resilience is grounded in the assurance that God is in control, even in the midst of suffering. This faith-based resilience enables individuals to withstand judgment and adversity, knowing that their worth and identity are secure in Christ.

Judgment, whether from others or ourselves, is a powerful force that can hinder personal growth and resilience. It creates barriers to self-expression, stifles creativity, and undermines the confidence needed to navigate life's challenges. However, by recognizing the destructive nature of judgment, we can begin to take steps to overcome it.

Fostering an environment of acceptance, empathy, and support is crucial for personal growth and resilience. This means surrounding ourselves with people who encourage us, rather than those who judge us. It also means cultivating self-compassion and learning to silence the internal critic that echoes the judgments of others.

For those who find strength in their faith, trusting in God's plan and relying on His promises can provide the resilience needed to overcome judgment and adversity. By leaning on scriptural truths and the examples of resilient believers, we can find the courage to continue growing and thriving, even in the face of judgment.

Ultimately, the journey of personal growth and resilience is one that requires both inner strength and external support. By shedding the weight of judgment and embracing the power of love, compassion, and faith, we can navigate our struggles with greater resilience and emerge stronger on the other side.

Empathy is a vital concept to grasp when it comes to understanding and supporting those who are struggling. To empathize fully with someone means to understand not just what they feel, but how they think—an understanding that requires both effort and development. Empathy goes beyond simply recognizing the surface-level emotions of another person; it involves a deep comprehension of the struggles they are going through and how these struggles affect their lives.

To begin with, empathy requires a genuine effort to understand why someone is behaving in a way that may initially seem confusing or frustrating. It's easy to rush to judgment when faced with behaviors we don't understand, but in moments like these, it's crucial to resist that impulse. Instead of judging, either to their face or to others, we should strive to put ourselves in their shoes and see the world from their perspective.

However, if we find ourselves unable to empathize fully with someone in their struggle, the next best thing we can do is simply to listen and show sympathy. Sometimes, being present and offering a non-judgmental space for someone to share their feelings can be more powerful than offering advice or trying to fix the situation. In times of crisis, people often need to feel heard and understood more than anything else.

Reducing judgment and increasing support within our communities is no small task, especially given that, as a society, we are often quick to judge. Our culture is steeped in judgmental attitudes, but if we hope to build stronger, more compassionate communities, we must find ways to counteract this tendency. One way to do this is by grounding our actions and interactions in love, empathy, and sympathy. We can look to the example of God the Son, who is described in Hebrews as our Sympathetic High Priest, able to empathize with our weaknesses and offer us mercy and grace in our times of need. This example reminds us that empathy should never be separated from truth, mercy, help, and grace.

To foster empathy, we can start by being kind and compassionate to one another, forgiving each other as Christ forgave us. In the Bible, we are urged to rejoice with those who rejoice and mourn with those who mourn and to be like-minded, sympathetic, loving, compassionate, and humble. These are not just religious ideals; they are practical guidelines for creating empathetic and supportive communities.

Practicing empathy in our daily lives involves a few key actions. First and foremost, it requires giving others our time—time to listen, time to understand, and time to be present with them in their struggles. Time is one of the most valuable things we can offer someone who is struggling, and it can make a world of difference.

Empathy also involves understanding the emotions that someone else is feeling and communicating that understanding back to them. This can be challenging, but it's essential if we want to connect with others on a deeper level. The more we practice perspective-taking, stay out of judgment, recognize others' emotions, and communicate our understanding, the more empathetic we become.

Addressing judgment in the context of personal struggle is crucial because judgment, when not grounded in understanding, can be harmful. To judge someone accurately, one must first understand them fully. Judgment, in its truest sense, involves making decisions or forming opinions based on wisdom, discretion, and good sense. However, when judgment is passed without understanding, it becomes a barrier to empathy and compassion.

A lack of empathy can hurt us deeply, leading to resentment, anger, and a host of other negative emotions. Being overly judgmental can close us off from others, making us bitter and less able to connect with those around us. In contrast, fostering empathy allows us to expand our worldview, release resentment, and ultimately find forgiveness, even for those with whom we might initially disagree.

Learning to become more empathetic takes time and practice, but it is well worth the effort. It involves becoming more curious about the people around us, seeing them as individuals rather than as members of a collective group, gaining direct experience with those who are different from us, and becoming better listeners. These practices help us to understand others more deeply and to approach them with compassion rather than judgment.

The broader implications of unchecked judgmental attitudes are significant. When judgment prevails, those in the midst of struggle may never find the support they need to heal and overcome their challenges. In the worst cases, judgment can lead to isolation, despair, and even death. Conversely, fostering empathy and reducing judgment can contribute to collective well-being by creating a more supportive and understanding society. Empathy brings with it the potential for freedom, love, and hope—elements that are essential for healing and growth.

Ultimately, it is important to remember that while we can strive to be empathetic and non-judgmental, the ultimate judgment belongs to God. The Bible speaks of various judgments, both for believers and unbelievers, but it also assures us that through faith in Christ, we can be freed from the judgment of sin. This understanding can serve as a reminder that our role is not to judge others harshly, but to approach them with the same mercy, grace, and empathy that we ourselves have received. By doing so, we can help to create a more compassionate and empathetic world, one where people feel supported in their struggles and encouraged to grow and heal.

CHAPTER SIX
MATERIALISM IN THE STRUGGLE

"Then he said to them, 'Watch out! Be on your guard against all kinds of greed; life does not consist in an abundance of possessions.'"

- Luke 12:15

In times of struggle, it's almost instinctual to reach for something tangible, something that we can hold or possess, as a source of comfort. The allure of materialism is powerful because it promises a quick fix, an easy distraction from the emotional or spiritual pain we might be enduring. Whether it's the thrill of buying a new gadget, the satisfaction of driving a shiny new car, or the fleeting pleasure of donning the latest fashion, these moments of acquisition can make us feel a sense of happiness, albeit temporary. Yet, this happiness is often a fleeting illusion, and before long, the cycle begins anew. The more we acquire, the more we desire, and the pursuit of material wealth becomes an endless loop that seems to offer relief but ultimately leaves us feeling more empty and disconnected than before.

Material possessions can certainly provide a momentary lift, a distraction from the hardships we face. In the midst of a personal or financial struggle, the act of purchasing something new or achieving a financial milestone might feel like a victory. It gives us something to focus on, a way to momentarily forget the emotional turmoil or existential dread that might be lurking beneath the surface. But this distraction, as comforting as it may seem, is just that—a temporary escape. The struggle remains, unresolved and in waiting, and no amount of material wealth or possessions can truly alleviate the deeper issues that trouble our hearts and minds.

The psychological grip of materialism is rooted in the way we, as a society, compare ourselves to others. From a young age, we are conditioned to measure our worth against external markers—what we own, where we live, the clothes we wear, and the gadgets we carry. These comparisons are particularly potent during times of struggle when we might feel vulnerable or inadequate. Material goods, then, become a way to bolster our self-esteem, to prove to ourselves and to others that we are successful, that we are keeping up in the unspoken competition of life. However, this pursuit is fraught with misconceptions and pitfalls. One of the most pervasive is the belief that material wealth equates to happiness. We see the luxurious lives of the wealthy and assume that their possessions bring them peace, contentment, and joy. Yet, research and real-life experiences often tell a different story.

Studies have shown that materialistic individuals tend to have lower life satisfaction and are more prone to depression. The more we rely on material possessions to fill the void within us, the more dissatisfied we become with our lives. The things we accumulate cannot provide the deep, lasting happiness we crave. Instead, they often leave us feeling even more empty and unfulfilled. This is because materialism directs our attention outward, toward the things of this world, rather than inward, where true contentment lies. The teachings of Jesus highlight this truth, reminding us that life does not consist in the abundance of possessions. The pursuit of material goods is a false promise, a distraction that diverts our attention from what truly matters. Rather than finding security and fulfillment, we find ourselves in a relentless chase, always wanting more but never finding enough.

Societal norms and the media play a significant role in perpetuating the myth that material wealth brings happiness. In American culture, success is often measured not by who we are or what we do, but by what we own. The media reinforces this narrative by glorifying wealth, luxury, and consumerism. Advertisements, television shows, movies, and social media are saturated with images of people living lavish lifestyles, surrounded by expensive possessions. This creates a powerful narrative that to be somebody and to be successful, one must accumulate things. This narrative is seductive, especially when we are struggling. It tells us that if we just had more if we could just buy that one more thing, we would be happier, more fulfilled, and more accepted by society.

But this is a dangerous lie. The more we buy into this narrative, the more we disconnect from our true needs—emotional, spiritual, and relational. Jesus' teachings remind us that our focus should not be on the things of this world but on the kingdom of God. When we prioritize material wealth, we lose sight of the deeper fulfillment that comes from living a life rooted in faith, love, and community. The things of this world are fleeting, and they can never truly satisfy the longing of the human soul.

One of the most insidious aspects of materialism is the way it creates a false sense of security. We are taught to believe that if we have enough money and enough possessions, we will be safe from harm, insulated from the struggles and uncertainties of life. But this is a dangerous misconception. Material possessions can never truly protect us from life's inevitable challenges. They cannot heal emotional wounds, mend broken relationships, or provide the deep sense of purpose that comes from living a life of meaning and integrity. The security that materialism offers is an illusion, one that can easily crumble when life's storms hit.

Materialism also fails to address the deeper emotional and spiritual needs that we all have. It is a mask, a way to avoid facing the real issues in our lives. But the more we rely on material goods, the deeper the pit we dig for ourselves. We become buried in our possessions and our debt, and the struggle, instead of being alleviated, grows even more overwhelming. The emotional toll of this pursuit can lead to despair, a darkness that material wealth can never light. We may find ourselves more isolated, more disconnected from others, and more distant from God.

Spiritually, materialism is equally destructive. It shifts our focus from God to ourselves, from the eternal to the temporary. We become self-reliant, thinking that we can buy our way out of struggle and that we can control our fate through the things we accumulate. But in doing so, we serve the wrong master. Jesus warned that we cannot serve both God and mammon and when we choose materialism, we choose a path that leads away from the true security and fulfillment that only God can provide. Materialism serves the wrong master, one that is demanding and unforgiving, one that can never truly satisfy the deepest longings of the human heart.

While materialism offers a tempting escape from the struggles of life, it is a deceptive one. It may provide temporary relief, a momentary distraction, but it ultimately leaves us feeling empty, disconnected, and unfulfilled. The pursuit of material wealth cannot satisfy the deeper needs of our souls. Instead of turning to things, we are called to turn to God, to seek first His kingdom, and to trust that in Him, we will find true peace and fulfillment. The things of this world are temporary, but the love and grace of God are eternal, and it is in Him that we find the true security and happiness we seek.

Materialistic behavior is often driven by deep-seated psychological mechanisms that compel individuals to seek comfort and fulfillment in possessions rather than addressing the root causes of their discontent. The pursuit of material wealth as a means to fill an emotional void is not a new phenomenon, but it has been greatly exacerbated by advancements in technology and the ease with which consumers can now acquire goods. The accessibility of both physical and online stores has made it easier than ever to indulge in this behavior, leading to an increase in compulsive buying habits. This tendency to associate personal well-being and success with the accumulation of possessions reflects a broader cultural narrative that equates material wealth with happiness. However, as research has shown, the satisfaction derived from such behavior is often short-lived, followed by feelings of regret and guilt.

The drive to acquire more and more possessions is often rooted in feelings of inadequacy, insecurity, and social comparison. In many cases, individuals turn to materialism as a coping mechanism, using retail therapy as a way to alleviate emotional distress. Unlike routine shopping trips that fulfill practical needs, retail therapy is emotionally driven, and triggered by feelings of depression, anxiety, or low self-worth. While occasional indulgence in retail therapy may provide temporary relief, it becomes problematic when it becomes a habitual response to emotional pain. This creates a vicious cycle where the act of shopping, intended to relieve stress, ultimately contributes to greater financial strain and emotional turmoil.

Consumer culture plays a significant role in reinforcing materialism as a coping mechanism. In a society where the pursuit of material wealth is glorified, individuals may turn to shopping as a way to escape negative emotions or to project an image of success. This behavior, however, is detrimental to mental health, as it distracts from the underlying issues that need to be addressed. The focus on acquiring more possessions as a means of achieving happiness or self-worth is ultimately a futile endeavor, as it does not address the root causes of dissatisfaction or emotional distress.

Societal expectations and pressures further reinforce materialistic values through various channels, including social media, advertising, and peer influence. Research suggests that materialistic individuals tend to be less happy, experiencing fewer positive emotions and higher levels of anxiety, depression, and substance abuse. Social media, in particular, has become a powerful force in shaping our perceptions of success and happiness. It allows individuals to create curated, often misleading, representations of their lives, projecting an image of wealth and success that may not reflect reality. This creates a feedback loop where individuals feel pressured to keep up with these exaggerated standards, leading to an obsession with material wealth and a disconnection from true, lasting fulfillment.

Advertising also plays a crucial role in perpetuating materialistic values by continuously promoting the idea that happiness and success can be achieved through the acquisition of goods. Advertisers craft narratives that suggest our lives will be better, more fulfilling, and more successful if we buy their products. This constant bombardment of consumerist messages reinforces the belief that material possessions are key to a happy and successful life, further entrenching materialism in our culture.

Cultural and societal values also shape our understanding of success and happiness, often equating them with material wealth. In American culture, the idea that this is the land of opportunity where anyone can achieve wealth and status is deeply ingrained. The prosperity gospel, a particularly influential segment of religious teaching, exacerbates this by promoting the notion that material success is a sign of divine favor. This unbiblical teaching has distorted the values of many, leading them to believe that their worth and success are measured by their material possessions.

This false narrative, promoted by both secular and religious institutions, blurs the line between genuine success and superficial wealth. It encourages individuals to prioritize material accumulation over spiritual and emotional well-being, leading to a hollow existence where the pursuit of wealth takes precedence over meaningful relationships, personal growth, and spiritual fulfillment. True success and contentment, as taught in Christian scripture, are not found in the accumulation of material goods but in the pursuit of spiritual blessings and treasures in heaven. The Bible teaches that life is short and that focusing on temporary, material things is ultimately futile. Real success lies in living a life aligned with God's will, where spiritual blessings are valued over material wealth.

In our modern world, the pursuit of material wealth is often equated with success and fulfillment. Advertisements, social media, and cultural norms all reinforce the idea that more money, a bigger house, a fancier car, and an abundance of possessions will lead to a better life. But the reality is far more complex. Beneath the surface of material abundance lies a darker truth—one that reveals the limitations of wealth as a source of true happiness.

The story of the Laodicean Christians, as recounted in the Bible, serves as a powerful reminder of the dangers of materialism. Despite their material wealth, they were spiritually destitute. Jesus rebuked them, pointing out that their riches had blinded them to their spiritual poverty. This ancient lesson resonates today, as countless individuals and communities continue to fall into the same trap—believing that money and possessions can fill the void that only spiritual and emotional fulfillment can satisfy.

One of the most striking modern examples of this is the rise of the prosperity gospel—a doctrine that has swept through many churches, particularly in the United States. The prosperity gospel teaches that material wealth and success are signs of God's favor, attainable by anyone who follows the right steps or donates the right amount. It promises a life of abundance but often delivers the opposite. Those who subscribe to this belief and fail to achieve the promised riches are left feeling inadequate and abandoned, convinced that they simply didn't do enough to earn God's favor.

The impact of the prosperity gospel extends far beyond the individual, creating ripple effects throughout entire communities. I once knew a couple who were devout members of a church that preached this doctrine. They were lured into a get-rich-quick scheme promoted by a fellow churchgoer, convinced that it was their path to financial freedom. Blinded by the promise of wealth, they ignored their mounting debts and the growing strain on their marriage. When the scheme inevitably collapsed, they were left not only financially ruined but also spiritually shattered. The embarrassment and sense of failure were too much to bear, and they eventually left the church, cutting themselves off from the community that had once been their support system.

Then there was David, a friend who struggled with mental health issues. Desperate for answers, he turned to the teachings of the prosperity gospel, believing that wealth would cure his problems and bring him happiness. But the more he acquired, the more empty he felt. His relentless pursuit of material success became an obsession, consuming him day and night. In the end, the pressure and disillusionment were too much, and David tragically took his own life. His story is a heartbreaking reminder of the emptiness that can accompany the single-minded pursuit of wealth.

These stories are not isolated incidents. They reflect a broader cultural phenomenon often referred to as "affluenza"—a painful, socially transmitted condition characterized by overload, debt, anxiety, and waste, all resulting from the relentless pursuit of more. Affluenza may be a modern term, but its effects are all too real. It is a condition that leaves people spiritually bankrupt, emotionally exhausted, and disconnected from what truly matters in life.

The term itself might be dismissed by some as a buzzword, but it encapsulates a deep truth about the corrosive effects of materialism. As people amass wealth, they often find that their relationships suffer, their health deteriorates, and their personal growth stalls. The constant pressure to maintain a certain lifestyle—to keep up with the Joneses—can lead to chronic stress, burnout, and a host of physical and mental health issues.

The long-term consequences of living a materialistic lifestyle are severe. While the initial allure of wealth might seem promising, the reality is that materialism often leads to a kind of death—a death of the soul, the spirit, and sometimes even the body. The stress of maintaining a facade of wealth can be overwhelming, leading to anxiety, depression, and in extreme cases, suicide.

Moreover, the relentless pursuit of wealth can create a profound sense of isolation. As people focus on acquiring more, they often neglect their relationships, becoming disconnected from their loved ones and their community. This isolation can lead to a downward spiral of loneliness and despair, as the very things they sought to avoid—emotional and spiritual emptiness—take hold of their lives.

The stories of those who have prioritized material wealth over well-being offer important lessons. They remind us that wealth, while valuable, is not a panacea. It cannot cure loneliness, mend a broken heart, or bring true peace of mind. On the contrary, when pursued at the expense of health, relationships, and personal growth, wealth can become a burden, robbing us of the very things that make life worth living.

True happiness and fulfillment come not from the accumulation of possessions, but from the richness of our relationships, the depth of our spiritual life, and the growth of our character. It is only by recognizing the limitations of materialism that we can begin to seek out what truly matters.

In the end, the pursuit of wealth is a deeply human endeavor, driven by a desire for security, status, and success. But when this pursuit becomes all-consuming, it can lead us down a path of destruction, leaving us spiritually and emotionally bankrupt. The challenge, then, is to find a balance—to appreciate the value of material wealth without allowing it to define our lives.

As we reflect on these stories and the lessons they offer, it becomes clear that success cannot be measured by wealth alone. True success is found in the strength of our relationships, the depth of our faith, and the integrity of our character. It is about living a life that is rich in meaning, purpose, and love—values that cannot be bought or sold, but must be cultivated and cherished. As you move forward in your own life, consider the ways in which you may have been influenced by the allure of materialism and ask yourself whether the price you pay is worth it. True wealth lies not in what you own, but in who you are and the connections you build with others.

There is only one true way to live a life of happiness, peace, joy, and love, and that is by seeking the true God, discovering His purpose for us, and following the journey He has planned for our lives. To live a life apart from materialism, one must know God's word and what it says about this topic. The Bible reminds us, "I am the Lord your God. You shall have no other gods before me." The trouble with materialism is that it seeks satisfaction in things, not in God. Jesus said, "Seek ye first the kingdom of God and His righteousness, and all these things shall be yours as well." (Matthew 6:33)

The fact that there are no alternatives to God's way is not complicated. However, if you must find a way to live apart from God's way—in other words, if you are not a believer—then you might consider living the life of a minimalist. This lifestyle is the alternative to the believer's path. Paradoxically, by owning less, the things we do bring greater joy to our lives.

When we declutter, all our possessions can become our favorite things, rather than just stuff that gets in the way. It's important to note that even the best followers of Christ can miss the mark when it comes to hiding behind their belongings. No one is immune to the problematic issue of materialism.

Cultivating emotional and spiritual well-being without relying on material possessions is a simple yet complex task. It requires knowing God's word and living a life based on it. Living simply, where less is more, is difficult in today's culture. Churches and cultural influences often push us to want more, to get more. Yet, true fulfillment lies in knowing God's purpose for us, and in prioritizing God, family, friends, and our community. Proverbs 16:11 offers insight into living a balanced life: "A just weight and balance are the Lord's; all the weights in the bag are His work." This proverb reminds us that everything belongs to God, and He is the standard by which we should measure our lives.

To live a fulfilling life, it's crucial to stop wanting more and start giving more of our time to those in need. We must avoid trying to keep up with people who don't truly matter. Authenticity is key—be real in all you do, and strive to be the person God created you to be. When you shift your focus from material wealth to personal growth, your happiness increases. You'll desire to be the person God intended you to be, and your mental and physical health will improve. Letting go of the pursuit of worldly riches and the fake reality portrayed on social media brings peace, harmony, and balance to life. When struggles arise—and they will—you'll be prepared to face them and emerge victorious.

Relationships are crucial to achieving lasting fulfillment. They not only contribute to a complete sense of fulfillment but also help develop lasting peace and harmony in your life. Relationships affect your choices, and your choices, in turn, affect your relationships. Be very careful about the relationships you cultivate, as they can either lead you toward materialism or help you maintain balance. Your community is the collective of your relationships, and they shape you into the person you are. Thriving relationships enhance your physical health, emotional well-being, financial stewardship, and ability to fulfill your life's work, increasing your peace, joy, and harmony.

Embracing minimalism or simplicity contributes to a more meaningful life by helping us be intentional about where our treasure is and, therefore, where our heart is. The Christian faith and minimalism go hand in hand. Jesus lived a simple, minimalist lifestyle, owning few possessions. Christian minimalism challenges our assumptions about what life should look like, cutting through society's lies and inviting us into the life Jesus calls us to live—one lived intentionally, free from physical, spiritual, and emotional busyness.

During difficult times, it is essential to resist the lure of materialism by changing how you perceive yourself and understanding the importance of your place in this world. Aside from extreme poverty, psychologists have found no connection between materialistic wants and happiness. Stay rooted in God's word and understand what it says about materialism. As 1 Timothy 6:6-11 advises, "For we brought nothing into this world, and it is certain we can carry nothing out. And having food and clothing, with these we shall be content. But those who desire to be rich fall into temptation and a snare, and into many foolish and harmful lusts which drown men in destruction and perdition."

Mindfulness, gratitude, and spiritual practices can help reduce reliance on material goods for happiness by aligning our understanding of the purpose of material wealth with God's intentions. There are four fundamental purposes for material wealth: to provide for basic needs, to confirm direction, to give to those in need, and to illustrate God's power and care in provision. Understanding these purposes allows us to see how materialism relates to God's work in our lives and communities. Gratitude for our existence and our place in life—whether in the struggle or at the top of the mountain—keeps us close to God and aware of our true purpose.

Redefining success and happiness is crucial in overcoming materialistic tendencies. Spiritual wealth, acquired through a relationship with God, leads to true happiness because it is a resource that will never run dry. Material wealth, on the other hand, is dependent on factors often beyond our control. Spiritual wealth is entirely within our grasp, and we determine how much or how little we have of it in our lives. Overcoming materialistic tendencies in today's culture is challenging, but it is achievable. We must be mindful of who we allow into our lives, what we watch, and what we accept as reality. Success should be measured not by material possessions, but by our spiritual wealth, self-worth, and alignment with God's purpose for our lives.

CHAPTER SEVEN
FAKE HAPPY IN THE STRUGGLE

"The LORD is close to the brokenhearted and saves those who are crushed in spirit." In a world that prizes appearances and success, it can be tempting to project an image of happiness even when we are struggling inside. This phenomenon, often referred to as "fake happiness," involves putting on a facade of contentment and well-being while concealing our true emotions and hardships. But what does it truly mean to be "fake happy," and how does it differ from genuine happiness?

Fake happiness is a state of emotional dissonance where one's outward expressions of joy and contentment are at odds with their internal reality. It's the smile plastered on a face that hides the pain underneath, the laughter that covers up tears, and the assurances of being "fine" when everything is far from it. Being fake in the struggle means not being true to yourself or to others. It's about living a double life—one that is presented to the world and another that remains hidden, often even from oneself.

This double life, however, comes with serious consequences. When we pretend to be happy, we deny ourselves the opportunity to confront and address the underlying issues causing our distress. Over time, this denial can take a toll on both our mental and physical health. We may begin to feel disconnected from ourselves and others, experience increased stress and anxiety, and even fall into depression as the gap between our public persona and private reality widens.

Genuine happiness, on the other hand, is not a facade but a reflection of true joy. It comes from an inward perspective of what is true and authentic within us. Genuine happiness is not something that can be faked or manufactured; it is a byproduct of joy, which is rooted in a deeper, spiritual sense of well-being. Joy is not something that we can produce on our own; it's a gift from God. His joy brings us peace in any struggle, and from that joy, genuine happiness naturally flows.

Genuine happiness does not require us to ignore or suppress our struggles. Instead, it allows us to embrace them with a sense of peace and assurance that transcends our circumstances. This kind of happiness is resilient because it is anchored in something deeper than the fleeting pleasures of life—it is grounded in the unshakeable joy that comes from a relationship with God. In contrast to fake happiness, which is superficial and temporary, genuine happiness is enduring and transformative.

Living a double life—where we present a happy exterior while hiding our struggles—can lead to a number of negative outcomes. Mentally, the effort to maintain this facade can be exhausting. It requires constant vigilance to ensure that our true feelings do not slip through the cracks. Over time, this can lead to increased stress, anxiety, and a sense of isolation, as we feel unable to share our true selves with others.

Physically, the stress of living a double life can manifest in a variety of ways, from tension headaches and fatigue to more serious conditions such as high blood pressure and heart disease. The body and mind are deeply connected, and when we are not true to ourselves emotionally, it can take a physical toll on our health.

Moreover, fake happiness can strain our relationships. When we are not honest about our struggles, we prevent others from truly knowing us and offering the support we need. This can lead to feelings of loneliness and disconnection, as well as a sense of being misunderstood or unsupported by those around us. True connection requires vulnerability, and vulnerability is impossible when we are hiding behind a mask of fake happiness.

To move from fake happiness to genuine happiness, we must first acknowledge the reality of our struggles. This requires courage and a willingness to be vulnerable, both with ourselves and with others. It also involves letting go of the need to maintain a perfect image and embracing the messiness and imperfection of life.

"To be yourself in a world that is constantly trying to make you something else is the greatest accomplishment."

– Ralph Waldo Emerson

Authenticity is key to genuine happiness. When we are honest about our struggles and allow others to see us as we truly are, we open the door to deeper connections and more meaningful relationships. We also allow ourselves to experience the full range of human emotions, rather than suppressing those that are uncomfortable or inconvenient.

Embracing authenticity does not mean that we must always be open about our struggles with everyone we meet. Rather, it means being true to ourselves and allowing ourselves to feel and express our emotions honestly, even if we choose to do so only with a trusted few. It means acknowledging that it is okay not to be okay and that we do not have to carry our burdens alone.

In the end, genuine happiness is not about avoiding or denying the struggles of life. It is about finding peace and joy in the midst of those struggles, trusting in the deeper truths that sustain us, and allowing our authentic selves to shine through. In doing so, we not only find true happiness for ourselves, but we also inspire and uplift those around us, creating a ripple effect of authenticity and joy in the world.

We all, at some point in our lives, feel compelled to wear a mask of happiness, especially when the reality of our emotions is anything but joyful. This compulsion often stems from a deep-seated fear—fear of judgment, fear of rejection, and fear of vulnerability. Society teaches us to value appearances and to present ourselves as strong and unshaken, even when we are crumbling inside. This need to maintain a facade can become so ingrained that we start believing in the image we project, even as it distances us from our true selves.

The act of putting on a facade is, in many ways, an act of self-preservation. We hide our pain because we fear that exposing it will make us appear weak or flawed. We worry that if others see our struggles, they will think less of us, or worse, turn away from us. So, we smile through the pain, laugh when we want to cry, and insist we're fine when we're anything but. This false portrayal of happiness, however, comes at a high cost.

In my own life, the need to project happiness while hiding my struggles was a recurring theme. This struggle is something I delve deeply into in my book, *The Invisible Soul, Rise Up*. The absence of genuine happiness in my life was something I knew all too well, but to the outside world, I appeared to be thriving. I had become a master at faking happiness, even when my world was falling apart. This chapter is crucial because it unveils the harmful consequences of living this double life and serves as a reminder that true healing begins with authenticity.

One of the earliest and most poignant examples of this facade in my life occurred during my grade school years. At home, I was subjected to severe abuse by a person who embodied cruelty. Every day was a battle for survival, yet each morning I put on a smile and went to school, determined not to let anyone see the pain I was enduring. My teachers, bless their hearts, would often comment on how cheerful I seemed. They saw a happy, well-adjusted child, but they had no idea that my smile was a mask hiding the bruises, both physical and emotional, that I carried.

The disconnect between my external appearance and internal reality was stark, but no one questioned it. It wasn't their fault—they only saw what I allowed them to see. My facade was so convincing that it even fooled the authorities. I recall a particularly harrowing incident when the neighbors, alarmed by the sounds of violence, called the police. When the officers arrived, they spoke briefly with the abuser and then turned to me. One of them said, "Just deal with it, it's part of life, son." Those words struck me like a blow. At that moment, I realized that my suffering was invisible to the world. No one saw the pain behind my smile. I was, in essence, an invisible soul—a child unseen by those who should have protected me, yet fully exposed to the cruelty of my tormentor.

As I grew older, the facade of happiness became a well-practiced habit. Even in situations where I should have felt safe and supported, I continued to hide my true feelings. Later in life, I was blessed with the opportunity to join a water sports ministry that traveled across America, teaching at-risk kids how to ski and sharing the message of Jesus with them. On the surface, it seemed like a dream come true—a chance to combine my love of water sports with a mission to help others. There were moments of real joy, times when I felt a genuine connection to the kids and to the work we were doing. But the cracks in my facade soon began to show.

I was supposed to be the beacon of happiness, the person who could inspire these kids by sharing how Jesus had brought joy into my life. But inside, I was struggling. The darkness I had carried with me since childhood was still there, gnawing away at me. The more I tried to project happiness, the more I felt like a fraud. My internal struggle was relentless, and it began to take a toll on me. The facade that had once protected me was now suffocating me.

It was during this time that I reached a breaking point. The weight of living a double life—preaching happiness while feeling anything but—became too much to bear. I was on the verge of collapse, emotionally and spiritually. But in that dark place, I found something unexpected: grace. I was surrounded by people who loved me, who saw through my facade and refused to let me continue living a lie. They taught me that it was okay to be unhappy, that it was okay to struggle, and that I didn't have to fake it anymore.

Their compassion and acceptance were a revelation to me. For the first time, I began to understand that true strength comes not from hiding our struggles but from facing them head-on. I learned that being authentic, even when it's painful, is the only path to true healing. It was in these moments of raw honesty with myself and others that I began to experience genuine happiness for the first time. The joy I had been preaching to others was no longer just words—it became a reality in my own life.

This journey from fake happiness to authenticity is something I continue to explore in *The Invisible Soul, Rise Up*. It's a journey that taught me that real happiness is not about being perfect or always having it together. It's about being true to who you are, even in the midst of struggle. It's about embracing the full range of human emotions—joy, pain, sorrow, and hope—and finding peace in the midst of it all. By sharing my story, I hope to encourage others to take off their masks and allow themselves to be seen, to be loved, and to find true joy in the process.

Fake happiness is rampant in today's society, permeating various aspects of our lives in ways that are often subtle but deeply impactful. I would go so far as to say that the majority of people are, at some level, engaged in this act of pretending to be happier than they truly are. The pressure to maintain a facade of contentment and success is immense, and it's not uncommon for people to feel disconnected from their true selves as they strive to project an image of happiness that doesn't align with their inner reality.

One of the most significant contributors to this phenomenon is the pervasive influence of social media. Platforms like Instagram, Facebook, and TikTok have created a culture where appearances often matter more than authenticity. On these platforms, people curate their lives to highlight only the most positive, attractive, and successful moments. This creates a distorted view of reality, where everyone else seems to be living a perfect life, leading to a constant comparison and a deep-seated insecurity for those who feel they don't measure up.

Social media doesn't just encourage the projection of fake happiness; it almost demands it. The pressure to present a picture-perfect life is so strong that it can make people feel compelled to hide their struggles, fears, and insecurities. The need for validation through likes, shares, and positive comments can drive people to manufacture a version of themselves that is more about pleasing others than being true to who they really are. It's a cycle that perpetuates itself: the more we see others projecting happiness, the more we feel we must do the same, even if it means sacrificing our authenticity.

But the problem isn't just confined to social media. Even in our day-to-day interactions, there's a noticeable decline in genuine connection. Have you noticed how rare it is for people to smile at each other in public, or to say simple, kind things like "Have a nice day" or "Thank you"? It's as if we've become so consumed with our own lives—our own projections of happiness—that we've lost the ability to engage in small acts of kindness that reinforce real human connection. The places where we gather, such as restaurants or coffee shops, often have employees hidden away behind counters or curtains, emphasizing efficiency over interaction. This detachment only feeds into the cycle of isolation and fake happiness.

Interestingly, this phenomenon isn't entirely new, though social media has certainly amplified it. When I was growing up, there were no online platforms to showcase one's life, but the pressure to appear happy was still very much present. We adapted to our surroundings, and the desire to be perceived as happy was strong even then. It's a fundamental human trait to seek happiness, but when that search becomes about projecting an image rather than finding true contentment, it can lead to a life of emptiness and disconnection.

The societal factors contributing to fake happiness are multifaceted. Beyond social media, there's a cultural emphasis on success, wealth, and appearance, all of which can push people to focus on external validation rather than internal fulfillment. The relentless pace of modern life leaves little room for introspection or genuine connection, leading people to settle for surface-level interactions and fleeting moments of happiness that don't satisfy the soul.

Throughout my life, there have been countless moments where the disparity between outward appearances and internal struggles has become painfully clear. For the majority of my life, I operated under a facade of strength and happiness, masking the true emotions churning beneath the surface. These experiences have become monumental in helping me recognize when I am slipping back into the habit of projecting an image that doesn't reflect my true self. It's been a long journey, but in recent years, I've come to understand the value of authenticity and the importance of being genuine, especially when I'm struggling.

Therapy has been a significant turning point for me in this regard. It has taught me that it's okay to be myself, even when I'm facing challenges. I've learned that it's not only acceptable but necessary to be transparent with those in my circle, to let them know when I'm not okay. This has profoundly impacted my ability to cope with difficult times. When I'm sad, I've learned to allow myself to be sad. When I'm down, it's okay to acknowledge that feeling. And when I'm in the midst of a struggle, I've discovered that it's crucial to reach out and let others know, so they can offer support. This level of honesty with myself and others has been transformative, allowing me to live more authentically and connect more deeply with the people around me.

As I've become more attuned to my own emotional landscape, I've also become more sensitive to the signs and behaviors that suggest someone else might be masking their true emotions with a "happy" facade. These signs are often subtle but telling. One of the most noticeable indicators is a blank stare—when you look into someone's eyes, and instead of seeing them, you see a reflection of something they're hiding. Those of us who have been in that place recognize this look instantly; it's like looking into a mirror of our past selves.

Another common sign is a lack of genuine engagement when in the company of others. They may be physically present, but there's a noticeable absence of attention or connection. They might laugh or seem to be participating in the conversation, but it's clear they're not truly there. Their mind is elsewhere, wrapped up in whatever struggle they're concealing. This detachment often goes unnoticed at first, but over time, it becomes more pronounced.

One of the most telling signs is a gradual withdrawal from their social circle. This can be a slow process, so subtle that it's only in hindsight that you realize how disconnected they've become. They stop attending gatherings, don't return calls or messages, and gradually fade from the group until one day, someone asks, "Where have they gone?" The response is usually something like, "They must be busy," but in reality, they're struggling and pulling away to hide it.

Then there's the fake laugh—a sound that anyone who's been there knows all too well. It's loud, often obnoxious, and devoid of any real joy. It's the kind of laugh that seems exaggerated and forced, going on too long as if trying to fill the emptiness inside. True laughter is contagious and full of life, but this kind of laughter is hollow, a clear indicator that something is wrong.

Finally, one of the most convincing behaviors of someone putting on a "happy" facade is their constant focus on themselves and their achievements. Conversations revolve around how great their life is, how successful their work is, and how much they have. It's as if they're trying to convince not only you but also themselves that everything is perfect. But the truth is, we're not always happy, and that's okay. When someone feels the need to project an image of being the best, the most successful, and the happiest all the time, it often signals that they are struggling with something deeper.

This phenomenon isn't just something I've observed in myself; I've seen it in others as well, both in personal relationships and within a broader societal context. Over the past few years, I've watched friends slowly withdraw from our social group. These were people we used to see regularly, who we talked with every week, shared meals with, and played together. But gradually, they've pulled away, isolating themselves as they try to navigate their struggles alone. It's heartbreaking to witness because I know how dangerous it can be to go through tough times without support.

These friends are still dear to us, and we respect their need for space, but we also make sure to let them know that we're here if they need us. A simple text now and then to check in, a reminder that they're not alone, can make all the difference. It's a delicate balance—giving them the room they need while also being a lifeline if they choose to reach out.

In reflecting on these experiences, I'm reminded of the words in Galatians 2:20,

"The Spirit is the indwelling wellspring of joy in God that we experience as we live by faith in the Son of God."

This passage beautifully encapsulates the connection between joy and faith, reminding us that true happiness comes not from external validation but from a deep, abiding relationship with God. It's a powerful reminder that genuine happiness isn't something we can fake; it's a gift that flows naturally from living in alignment with our faith and our true selves.

In today's society, the pressure to appear happy has become almost a prerequisite for social acceptance. This expectation is so deeply ingrained that any deviation from it is often seen as abnormal or even undesirable. From a young age, people are taught to equate happiness with success, stability, and worthiness. As a result, many individuals internalize the belief that if they aren't happy, something must be wrong with them. This societal norm drives people to suppress their true emotions, forcing them to adopt a facade of happiness to fit in.

The phrase "fake it until you make it" perfectly encapsulates this cultural expectation. It suggests that happiness is something that can be achieved simply by pretending and that if you just maintain the act long enough, genuine happiness will eventually follow. This mentality discourages authentic self-expression and reinforces the idea that vulnerability or sadness are signs of weakness. Consequently, individuals are pressured to conform to an unrealistic standard of perpetual happiness, even when they are struggling internally.

The advent of social media has only exacerbated this issue. Platforms like Instagram, Facebook, and TikTok have created an environment where people carefully curate their lives to showcase only the most positive and enviable moments.

These platforms encourage the sharing of glossy, edited snapshots that present an idealized version of reality, contributing to a distorted perception of what life is supposed to be like. In this world, happiness is constant, and struggles are invisible.

Social media inherently encourages comparison. As people scroll through their feeds, they are bombarded with images of others seemingly living perfect lives—traveling to exotic destinations, achieving career milestones, and celebrating picture-perfect relationships. This constant exposure to others' highlight reels can foster feelings of inadequacy and dissatisfaction with one's own life. The desire to keep up with these idealized images drives individuals to project a similarly polished and happy facade, even when their true circumstances are far from perfect.

Moreover, social media rewards the presentation of happiness. The instant gratification of likes, comments, and shares creates a feedback loop where people feel validated for their fake happy personas. The more positive feedback they receive, the more they feel compelled to continue the charade, even at the expense of their mental well-being. Over time, this can lead to a disconnection from reality, as individuals begin to measure their worth by the number of likes or followers they have, equating social media success with personal success.

The pressure to maintain a perfect, happy image can have devastating effects on both mental health and relationships. When individuals constantly suppress their true emotions to present a facade of happiness, they deny themselves the opportunity to process and address their genuine feelings.

This dissonance between their internal reality and external presentation can lead to emotional exhaustion, anxiety, and depression. The constant act of pretending can create a deep sense of isolation, as individuals may feel that no one truly understands or accepts their real selves.

Living inauthentically also erodes self-esteem. When people feel that they must be someone they're not to be accepted or loved, they internalize the belief that their true self isn't good enough. This internal conflict can lead to a fragmented sense of identity, where individuals feel disconnected from who they really are. In extreme cases, the pressure to maintain a fake happy persona can contribute to the development of serious mental health issues, including chronic stress and suicidal thoughts.

Relationships are equally affected by this societal pressure. When people aren't honest about their feelings, it creates barriers to true intimacy and connection. Friends and loved ones may feel that they don't know the person behind the facade, leading to feelings of distance and mistrust. The person putting on the happy face may also withdraw from relationships, fearing that their true emotions will be rejected or misunderstood. This withdrawal can lead to a breakdown in relationships, as the lack of authenticity and vulnerability prevents meaningful connections.

In this context, the pressure to appear happy becomes not just an individual challenge but a societal issue that affects the collective mental health and well-being. The emphasis on projecting happiness at all costs, driven by societal norms and amplified by social media, creates an environment where authenticity is sacrificed for the sake of appearance. The antidote lies in fostering a culture of authenticity, where people feel safe to express their true emotions without fear of judgment or rejection. Only by challenging these societal norms can we create a world where people are free to be themselves, and where true happiness—rooted in genuine self-acceptance—can flourish.

In a world where societal pressures often push us to conform to an idealized version of happiness, the journey toward authentic emotional expression and self-acceptance is both challenging and essential. To foster genuine emotional expression, one must first silence the inner critic—the small, insidious voice that whispers negativity and doubt into our minds. This voice, often born out of societal expectations and cultural norms, convinces us that our true selves are not enough. It tells us that we must constantly strive for happiness that is often unattainable and unrealistic.

True self-acceptance begins when we stop listening to this voice and start embracing who we are, flaws and all. It involves rejecting the cultural narrative that happiness is the ultimate measure of success and instead finding contentment in our true selves. To live authentically, we must cultivate self-compassion, recognizing that we are worthy of love and happiness just as we are. This means being kind to ourselves, acknowledging our struggles, and accepting that it's okay not to be happy all the time.

Forgiveness also plays a crucial role in this process. We must forgive not only those who have hurt us but also ourselves for the times we have tried to be someone we're not. Surrounding ourselves with a peer group of like-minded, authentic individuals can provide the support and encouragement needed to remain true to ourselves. These relationships can act as a buffer against societal pressures, allowing us to express our emotions honestly without fear of judgment.

Above all, finding true happiness requires looking beyond ourselves and turning to a higher power. For those of faith, this might mean seeking solace in the teachings and character of Jesus Christ. In His love and grace, we can find real joy—a joy that isn't dependent on external circumstances but is rooted in a deep, spiritual connection. By aligning our lives with His example, we can experience a profound sense of peace and fulfillment that transcends the superficial happiness often glorified by society.

For those struggling to maintain a facade of happiness, the first step is acknowledging that it's okay to not be okay. Life is complex and full of challenges, and pretending to be happy all the time only creates a disconnect between our true selves and the world around us. Embracing our authentic selves means letting go of the fear of judgment and accepting that our worth isn't determined by others' perceptions. It involves understanding that we were created with unique journeys and that our value lies not in how happy we appear but in how genuinely we live our lives.

God's teachings provide a roadmap for finding true happiness. His commandments guide us toward loving relationships, a healthy community, and a spirit of unselfishness—all of which contribute to a deep and lasting sense of joy. By living in alignment with these principles, we can break free from the societal expectations of constant happiness and find contentment in a life lived authentically.

Challenging societal expectations of perpetual happiness begins with mindfulness. It's important to regularly assess our thoughts and feelings, questioning why we feel the need to present a certain image to the world. Diving into God's Word can offer clarity and guidance, helping us to discern what truly brings happiness. The Beatitudes from the Gospel of Matthew, for example, provide powerful insights into the attitudes and mindsets that lead to true happiness. These teachings encourage us to find strength in humility, comfort in mourning, and fulfillment in seeking righteousness.

Reflecting on our own experiences with "fake happiness" is another crucial step in this journey. By examining the moments when we've felt compelled to wear a mask, we can begin to understand the impact this has had on our mental health and relationships. Are our desires rooted in real, meaningful connections, or are they tied to the superficial, fleeting validation that comes from projecting an image of happiness? This reflection can lead to a deeper understanding of ourselves and our true needs.

The message I hope readers take away from this chapter is the importance of authenticity. In a culture that often prioritizes appearance over substance, being true to oneself is a radical act. It's okay to be who you are, even if that doesn't align with societal expectations. Don't be afraid to seek help when needed, and remember that true happiness isn't something you need to manufacture—it's something that comes naturally when you live in alignment with your true self and God's plan.

Challenging the notion of "fake happiness" can lead to profound personal growth and self-understanding. Each time we reject the pressure to conform to this ideal, we strengthen our sense of self and deepen our connection to what truly matters. By embracing our authentic emotions, we create a life that is not only more fulfilling for ourselves but also brings joy to others and honors God. In doing so, we experience the true happiness that comes from living a life of integrity and purpose, guided by love, compassion, and faith.

CHAPTER EIGHT

DEATH AND BEAUTY IN THE STRUGGLE

To find beauty in the struggle of facing death is to uncover a grace that emerges amid the pain and turmoil. Death, often shrouded in fear and sorrow, can also be a deeply meaningful event marked by profound transformation. While pain and struggle are undeniably difficult, they can lead to a deeper appreciation of life's fleeting nature. This process reveals a form of beauty that emerges from the struggle itself. For some, death is not merely an end but a release—a moment of liberation from the trials of a terminal illness or a prolonged health crisis. This liberation brings a sense of peace and resolution, transforming the final moments into something profoundly beautiful.

From this perspective, death is seen as a passage to a new existence rather than just a struggle. The idea that one's soul will find peace in an eternal resting place provides comfort and a sense of beauty in the face of death. As Revelation 21:4 promises,

"He will wipe away every tear from their eyes, and death shall be no more, neither shall there be mourning, nor crying, nor pain anymore, for the former things have passed away."

This verse envisions death as a transition to a state of eternal peace, where the struggles of earthly life are left behind.

Confronting our mortality or that of a loved one can reveal an unexpected form of beauty and peace. This revelation often comes from a deep sense of understanding and acceptance. For those who believe in Jesus, death is not the end but a passage to a promised paradise. This belief can imbue the final moments with an extraordinary serenity. Consider the moment Jesus spoke to the thief on the cross, offering comfort with the promise:

"Truly, I say to you, today you will be with me in paradise"

\- Luke 23:43

This assurance provided the thief with peace even in his last moments.

The simplicity of finding beauty and peace in the face of death lies in understanding that life is a journey with a predetermined endpoint. What truly matters is how we live and prepare ourselves for the inevitable. Embracing the notion that death is a part of life's natural cycle allows us to appreciate its beauty and the peace that accompanies it. In the end, confronting mortality with faith and acceptance can transform the experience of dying from a struggle into a serene and beautiful passage. The struggle itself becomes a testament to the beauty of life's full circle, leading to a final peace that is both profound and comforting.

Facing death can often lead to profound personal growth and spiritual awakening. Stories of individuals who have confronted their mortality reveal how such experiences can lead to unexpected beauty and peace, offering deep insights into the human spirit.

Consider Keith's story, a testament to the transformative power of facing death with faith and purpose. Keith was a man who lived with a vision and a sense of purpose, marked by his unwavering commitment to his dreams and his deep connections with others. He saw life as a journey with a predetermined end, and he embraced it with a sense of acceptance and hope. In his final days, Keith's focus remained on the beauty of life and the legacy he wished to leave behind.

Hebrews 6:16-20 provides a comforting perspective on the nature of God's promises, offering assurance and hope even in the face of death. It describes how God's unchangeable promises act as an anchor for the soul, leading us through the challenges of life and into the sanctuary of eternal peace. This passage reflects the confidence that Keith carried with him as he approached the end of his life, knowing that his soul was anchored in the promise of eternal peace.

Keith's story is one of resilience and grace. He was a man who lived passionately and dreamed boldly, never letting the trials of life overshadow his vision. Keith's perspective on life and death was shaped by his experiences and his unwavering belief in the power of dreams and human connection. Despite the hardships he faced, he never spoke negatively about his past or his circumstances. Instead, he focused on the present and the future, encouraging others to learn, love, and live fully.

As Keith approached the end of his life, he continued to engage deeply with his beliefs and his quest for understanding. His final conversations with friends were marked by a search for meaning and a desire to grasp the essence of his faith. Keith's willingness to confront these profound questions with honesty and openness exemplified his commitment to personal growth and spiritual awakening.

In his last conversations, Keith expressed a sense of searching and seeking, reflecting a deep introspection about his faith and his understanding of Jesus. I shared a poignant exchange where I reassured Keith that the essence of faith is not always about complete understanding but about belief and trust. Keith's response was filled with love and acceptance, demonstrating his inner peace and the comfort he found in his spiritual journey.

Keith's story highlights how confronting mortality can lead to a profound sense of peace and clarity. His legacy, marked by his love, compassion, and integrity, continues to inspire others to live with purpose and to embrace life's challenges with grace. Keith's experience underscores the idea that even as we face the end of our lives, we can find beauty and meaning in our journey, leaving a lasting impact on those around us.

Ultimately, Keith's perspective on life and death transformed through his experience, leading him to a place of peace and fulfillment. His story serves as a powerful reminder that facing death with faith and purpose can lead to a profound sense of peace and beauty, offering a legacy of inspiration and love for those who continue to walk the path of life.

The awareness of mortality can serve as a profound catalyst for personal transformation. When we acknowledge that our time on earth is limited, it often prompts a re-evaluation of what truly matters. This realization can inspire us to invest more deeply in the things that hold genuine significance, rather than chasing after superficial goals or maintaining a façade of happiness.

Recognizing that we are born to die can lead to a profound shift in priorities. Many people spend their lives constructing a false image of success and contentment, masking their true selves behind a veneer of societal expectations. The awareness of mortality can strip away these illusions, compelling us to confront our authentic selves and embrace a more meaningful existence. We might find ourselves questioning what truly brings us joy and fulfillment, leading us to focus on relationships, love, and personal growth rather than materialistic pursuits.

When someone confronts the reality of death, several specific changes and realizations often occur. The shift from a façade to authenticity becomes apparent. The pretense of a perfect life gives way to a more honest and vulnerable expression of one's true feelings and desires. This process often involves shedding the distractions and superficialities that previously consumed our attention.

A person facing death might also experience a reduction in the importance placed on external achievements and possessions. The focus shifts from accumulating more to appreciating what is already present—cherishing meaningful relationships and savoring moments of connection and love. The realization of life's brevity encourages us to clear our schedules of less significant concerns, freeing up time to invest in what truly matters. This might mean prioritizing time with loved ones, pursuing passions that bring genuine satisfaction, or engaging in acts of kindness and compassion.

Ultimately, the awareness of mortality encourages a more authentic and intentional approach to life. It prompts us to live more fully, embracing what is truly important and letting go of what no longer serves our deeper purpose. By confronting the reality of death, we are offered the opportunity to transform our lives, making choices that reflect our true values and aspirations. This transformation can lead to a richer, more fulfilling existence, marked by genuine connections and a deeper appreciation for the fleeting nature of our time on earth.

Supporting someone who is grieving or dealing with loss requires a compassionate and patient approach. Even though we may not fully understand their pain, our presence can be a powerful form of support. The essence of being there for someone in mourning lies in simply offering a listening ear and a comforting presence. This approach is often termed "just being there." Sometimes, there is no need for words or solutions—just sitting quietly, offering a shoulder to lean on, and showing that you care can be immensely comforting. Grief is already a profound and complex experience, and additional drama or attempts to fix the situation can be counterproductive. The core of support is to offer love and understanding, allowing the bereaved to process their emotions in their own time.

These practical strategies of providing simple presence and empathy can help individuals find peace during their grieving process. Peace in the midst of loss often comes from the mercy and grace extended by friends and loved ones. This compassionate support mirrors the divine peace and comfort described in spiritual teachings, which can provide solace and strength to those who are grieving.

Experiencing loss can lead to a deeper understanding of life and spirituality. The realization of life's brevity and the inevitability of death can prompt profound reflections on our existence and purpose. Understanding that life is finite encourages a focus on what truly matters, such as relationships and spiritual connections. This awareness often leads to a search for a higher meaning or encounter with the divine, bringing a sense of peace and acceptance regarding the end of life. As Romans 8:38-39 emphasizes, nothing can separate us from the love of God, reinforcing the idea that spiritual connection provides comfort and reassurance even in the face of death.

Different cultures and belief systems offer various approaches to finding beauty in death. These perspectives often reflect how people cope with loss and find meaning in the life that was lived. Some cultures view death as a transition to a new phase of existence or rebirth, celebrating it as part of a larger spiritual journey. However, in the context of this book, the focus is on the belief in a singular divine truth as outlined in Christian teachings. According to the Gospel of John, faith in God provides a foundation for peace and understanding amidst life's trials.

From diverse perspectives, several lessons can be gleaned. While cultural and religious approaches to death offer valuable insights, they can also introduce confusion when many paths are presented as viable. The multiplicity of beliefs can sometimes lead to uncertainty and a false sense of hope. In navigating these diverse views, it's crucial to seek clarity and grounding in one's faith and understanding of the divine, rather than being swayed by conflicting interpretations. This approach helps to maintain a coherent and meaningful perspective on life and death, ensuring that one's beliefs and practices offer genuine comfort and guidance.

Community and support play crucial roles in helping individuals navigate grief and loss. Grief is a deeply human emotion that brings significant pain and suffering. During such times, a personal community becomes an essential pillar of support, offering hope and relief. This network of friends, family, and acquaintances can provide comfort, share memories, and offer practical assistance. Their presence alone can ease the burden of grief, helping individuals feel less isolated and more connected in their sorrow.

Cultivating a supportive environment for those experiencing loss involves fostering a community that prioritizes empathy and presence. This means actively engaging with those who are grieving, providing a listening ear, and offering genuine companionship. It's about creating a space where individuals feel safe to express their emotions without judgment. Building such a supportive environment requires an understanding that grief is a personal journey, and the best way to help is often to simply be there and offer support in whatever form is needed.

Facing one's own mortality can profoundly inspire changes in behavior, relationships, and life priorities. The realization of our finite existence often brings clarity about what truly matters. When confronted with the reality of death, people may shift their focus towards deepening relationships, reassessing their behavior, and prioritizing meaningful life goals. Recognizing that life is temporary can prompt individuals to invest more in their relationships with family, and friends, and their spiritual beliefs, as these become more apparent as central to a fulfilling life.

Examples of such changes include mending broken relationships, prioritizing time with loved ones, and focusing on personal growth. When one faces the prospect of their own mortality, trivial grievances, and material pursuits often lose their significance. Instead, the emphasis shifts towards nurturing love, peace, and harmony. This shift manifests in actions such as reconciling with estranged family members, expressing appreciation to friends, and living with a greater sense of purpose.

Key elements that contribute to a transformative experience when dealing with death or loss include achieving inner peace and accepting the reality of death as a natural part of life. Knowing that a loved one has moved on to a better place, free from pain, can bring solace. Philippians 1:23-24 reflects this sentiment, expressing the desire to be with Christ as far better than remaining in the flesh. This peace of mind can foster personal growth and acceptance, helping individuals come to terms with the inevitability of death and the changes it brings.

The interaction of these elements—acceptance, inner peace, and the understanding of death as a natural progression—fosters personal growth and a deeper appreciation of life. Grief and loss can lead to profound personal development, as individuals confront and work through their emotions. This process often opens new avenues for growth, allowing for a greater understanding of life's impermanence and the value of relationships.

Reconciling the pain of loss with the beauty of the memories left behind involves reflecting on the positive aspects of the deceased's life and the moments shared. Memories serve as a bridge between pain and peace, providing a way to honor the life lived and find solace in the love that remains. Practices such as creating memorials, sharing stories, and engaging in activities that celebrate the life of the departed can help in this reconciliation.

Reflecting on spiritual teachings can also aid in this process. For instance, the Gospel of John emphasizes the power of perfect love to cast out fear, suggesting that understanding and embracing divine love can transform the experience of loss. By focusing on the eternal love of God and the promise of an afterlife, individuals can find comfort and a renewed sense of purpose, which helps reconcile the pain of loss with the beauty of the memories left behind.

CHAPTER NINE

FAITH IN THE STRUGGLE

When we speak of faith, we often imagine something intangible, something rooted in belief, hope, and trust. But faith is more than just a fleeting emotion or a comforting thought—it is a powerful force that sustains and strengthens us in the most difficult of times. For me, faith has been the cornerstone of my resilience, especially during life's darkest hours. It is a gift, not earned by works, but given by God himself, and it is this gift that has been my refuge in struggle.

To truly grasp the significance of faith, we must go back to its origins. Faith, in the Christian context, is not something we muster up on our own; it's something bestowed upon us by God, a divine grace that allows us to trust in Him when all else fails. Martin Luther captured this truth in his doctrine of sola fide, or justification by faith alone, emphasizing that our salvation comes not through our own efforts, but through this faith granted by God. In his words, "If this article stands, the church stands; if this article collapses, the church collapses." The magnitude of this statement reflects the centrality of faith in the Christian life—it is the foundation upon which everything else rests.

Understanding faith in this way means recognizing that it's not a human endeavor. As Ephesians 2:8–9 says, "By grace you have been saved through faith; and that not of yourselves, it is the gift of God; not as a result of works, so that no one may boast." Faith is God's gift to us, something He imparts, not something we can earn or produce through our own strength. It is this divine gift that has carried me through the struggles I've faced, both in my personal life and in moments where everything seemed lost.

There have been times when the weight of life seemed unbearable—moments of despair, loss, and hardship where I questioned my ability to keep moving forward. In those moments, faith was not just a comforting idea but a lifeline. It wasn't my own strength that pulled me through, but the unwavering trust in a trustworthy person—Jesus Christ. As scripture teaches, "No one can come to Me unless the Father who sent Me draws him" (John 6:44). This means that in our darkest hours, it is God who draws us near, giving us the faith to believe, to trust, and to persevere.

Faith doesn't eliminate struggles; rather, it gives us the strength to endure them. It allows us to place our burdens at the feet of Christ, knowing that He will carry us through. When I think about the difficult times I've faced, whether it was the chaos of growing up in a broken home or the uncertainty of navigating adulthood without my father, it was my faith that provided a sense of stability in the midst of turmoil. Faith is not passive; it's an active trust in the One who holds all things together.

The beauty of faith is that it brings hope even when the future seems bleak. As Hebrews 11:1 tells us, "Now faith is the substance of things hoped for, the evidence of things not seen." In the midst of my struggles, I've often clung to this hope, knowing that there is a greater plan beyond what I can see. Faith has been my constant companion, reminding me that even when life feels overwhelming, God's grace is sufficient, and His promises are sure.

In every trial, I've found that faith is not just about believing in God's existence, but about trusting in His goodness, His love, and His sovereignty over every aspect of my life. It's easy to have faith when everything is going well, but it's in the struggle where true faith is tested and refined. It's in those moments of pain and uncertainty that I've learned to lean not on my own understanding, but on the faith that has been given to me—a faith that is anchored in Christ.

Looking back, I can see how each struggle has deepened my faith, drawing me closer to God and teaching me to rely on Him in ways I never thought possible. The challenges I've faced have not only strengthened my character but have also reminded me that I am not in control—God is. And it is through faith that I've been able to release my fears, trust in His plan, and walk forward with hope.

Faith, in the end, is about trusting in a God who is bigger than our struggles, a God who walks with us through the valleys and brings us out on the other side. For me, faith has been the key to resilience, the anchor that holds firm even in life's most violent storms. Without it, I don't know how I would have made it through. But with it, I've learned that no matter how difficult the struggle, there is always hope for tomorrow, because my faith rests in the One who never fails.

In times of struggle, faith is not just a belief—it is an act of trust in a Savior who sees our pain, understands our struggles, and promises to carry us through them. And for me, that faith has been and always will be, my greatest strength.

Faith has a way of molding us, shaping us into stronger, more resilient people than we ever thought possible. While many moments in my life have tested the limits of my strength, it's in those same moments that my faith has grown and led me to a deeper understanding of trust, hope, and divine grace.

Through the trials, I've come to see faith not just as a belief system, but as a lifeline—something that holds us together when everything else seems to fall apart.

One of the most significant trials in my life, where faith truly became the bedrock of my strength, was when my wife Lisa was diagnosed with cancer. That single word—cancer—has the power to stop you in your tracks, to strip away any semblance of control you think you have. It was a moment that challenged not just my faith, but my entire understanding of life and the future we had envisioned together. The initial shock of the diagnosis left us both reeling, questioning how we would navigate the days ahead.

I wish I could say that our first reaction was to fall on our knees and pray, but that wouldn't be the truth. Like anyone would, we immediately fell into the spiral of "what ifs." What are we going to do? How are we going to get through this? Fear, anxiety, and worry began to take over, and we found ourselves facing the overwhelming uncertainty that cancer brings. The mind starts to wander into dark places, focusing on all the worst-case scenarios, and the weight of that fear can feel unbearable.

But that mindset didn't last long. We soon realized that if we continued down the path of worry, it would only lead us further into despair. So we turned back to the one place where we knew we could find real peace—God. In that moment of surrender, we prayed. We asked God for the strength to endure, for the faith to trust Him with whatever the outcome might be. It wasn't easy, but we knew that God's plan was bigger than anything we could understand, and it was that trust in Him that began to replace the anxiety with a deep, abiding peace.

This peace didn't come because we believed everything would turn out perfectly. In fact, part of our prayer was acknowledging that we didn't know what the future held. We simply asked for God's presence, His strength, and His grace to carry us through whatever lay ahead. Whether Lisa would recover fully or not, we placed our trust in God, knowing that He would take care of her in the way that was best—whatever that might look like.

What I've learned from that experience is that faith doesn't mean we won't face hardship. It doesn't mean that life will be smooth or free from pain. What it does mean is that in the midst of those trials, we are never alone. Faith gave us the strength to face Lisa's cancer head-on, not with fear, but with hope. It allowed us to rest in the knowledge that God is sovereign and that, no matter what happens, He is good. That faith brought a peace that nothing else could offer, and it was that peace that carried us through some of the most difficult days of our lives.

This experience reinforced what I had long believed but hadn't fully grasped until then: faith is not about controlling the outcome, but about trusting the One who controls it all. It is about surrendering our fears, our worries, and our need for certainty, and resting in the promises of a loving God who knows what we need better than we do.

Before I was given the gift of faith, my response to challenges was very different. In those early years, I leaned entirely on my own understanding and strength. I thought I could navigate life's difficulties with sheer willpower and human effort. But time and again, I found myself falling short.

My efforts, more often than not, ended in frustration, failure, and a sense of hopelessness. Without faith, life felt like a constant uphill battle with no end in sight.

It wasn't until I encountered the truth of Jesus Christ that I began to understand what real hope and strength looked like. My personal journey, much of which I've shared in *The Invisible Soul, Rise Up*, speaks to the power of faith in transforming not just the way we see the world, but how we approach adversity. Missing the foundational pieces in my formative years left me vulnerable to the world's solutions for dealing with hardship. I tried to overcome struggles on my own terms, only to find that human strength was not enough.

One of the most significant turning points in my life came after enduring trauma at the hands of people who meant only harm. The weight of that abuse left deep scars, not just physically but emotionally and spiritually as well. There were days when I wondered if I would ever truly heal, if I would ever rise above the pain that had been inflicted upon me. The world offered temporary fixes—distractions, self-reliance, and empty promises of healing through my own effort—but none of those solutions provided real peace.

It wasn't until I turned to the Cross that I found true healing. Only in Jesus did I find the strength to not just endure the pain, but to overcome it. Faith led me to a place of surrender, where I could let go of the hurt and trust in God's redemptive power. It was through faith that I realized healing wasn't something I could achieve on my own—it was something God could bring about in me, through His grace and love. The Cross became a symbol not just of Christ's suffering, but of the hope and freedom that comes through faith in Him.

In every trial I've faced, faith has been the anchor that holds me steady. Whether it's facing the unknown with Lisa's diagnosis, or overcoming the trauma of my past, faith has provided the strength, resilience, and peace that I could never have found on my own. It's not just a belief; it's a way of living, a constant reminder that no matter what life throws at me, I am never alone.

Faith has been my greatest source of growth and freedom, and it's this faith that has given me hope for the future—even when that future is uncertain. Whether beautiful or difficult, I trust in God's plan, knowing that He will carry me through it all.

When reflecting on the pivotal moments in my life that have tested my faith, one of the first that comes to mind is the early years of raising our daughters, Sara and Laura. At that time, Lisa and I had an awareness of God—He was more of a distant concept than a close and present help. We believed in God, and we knew of Jesus, but there was a crucial piece missing: we hadn't met Him personally. Raising two young girls in a world where God was only a vague notion terrified us. We were navigating parenthood with the weight of that uncertainty, wondering how we could guide them in a world that seemed increasingly hostile to the idea of faith.

Looking back, I see that those years were preparing me for a pivotal moment—one that would change the course of my life and my family's lives. Five years after our girls were born, Lisa and I found ourselves sitting in a church, hearing for the first time about the personal, loving God who wanted to know us deeply. It wasn't just an intellectual understanding of who God is; it was an introduction to the very heart of faith—trusting in a relationship with Jesus Christ. At that moment, we realized that raising a family based only on a distant acknowledgment of God would never be enough. We needed a faith that was active, real, and transformative.

That realization marked a turning point for me. The thought of raising Sara and Laura without a firm foundation in faith felt like building a house on sand. It was terrifying, but it was also a wake-up call. It led me to seek a deeper understanding of faith—not just for myself, but for my family. This was the beginning of my journey toward a faith that wasn't just an idea but a daily practice of trust in God, especially when faced with the inevitable struggles that life would bring.

Faith, I've learned, is a journey of growth. It doesn't come fully formed but rather develops through each trial and experience. Every challenge—whether it be financial, health-related, or relational—has provided an opportunity for my faith to deepen. And with each step, trusting in Jesus, the most trustworthy person, has brought about growth. This trust didn't just help me survive those struggles; it helped me thrive in the midst of them. With every hardship, I found that my understanding of life and its purpose became clearer, and my reliance on God became stronger.

One of the most profound lessons I've learned is that faith and hope are intricately connected. Hope is often seen as something future-oriented, but it is also a reflection of the faith we've held in the past. Faith is the trust we place in God, and hope is the belief that this trust will continue to guide us forward. In times of struggle, hope becomes the anchor we hold onto, even when the waves of life threaten to sweep us away. But it's important to remember that hope, like faith, is not always steady—it can waver, shift, and sometimes feel distant. That's why our faith must remain constant, grounded in Jesus.

Faith has influenced my approach to overcoming obstacles in ways I couldn't have imagined before. It's no longer about relying on my own strength or wisdom; it's about turning to the One who holds the future in His hands. Trusting in Jesus has become my default response to adversity, not because I'm immune to fear or doubt, but because I've seen time and again that He is faithful. His presence in the midst of my struggles has given me a peace that transcends understanding, a peace that doesn't depend on the circumstances but on the certainty of His goodness.

When Lisa and I faced financial difficulties early in our marriage, we felt the weight of uncertainty bearing down on us. In those moments, the temptation to rely on our own resources was strong, but we quickly realized that our efforts alone weren't enough. Faith taught us to trust in God's provision, even when we couldn't see a way out. It wasn't always easy—there were moments of doubt, moments when we wondered if we would make it through. But each time we surrendered our worries to God, He provided in ways we couldn't have anticipated. Sometimes it was through unexpected financial support; other times, it was through the strength to persevere when things seemed bleak.

This same faith has been the foundation in maintaining hope throughout my life. I've learned that faith doesn't guarantee a life without challenges; it guarantees that we won't face those challenges alone. Faith is the assurance that God is with us, no matter the outcome. And hope? Hope is the belief that no matter how dark things may seem, there is always light on the other side of the struggle. Faith gives us the strength to hold on when everything else tells us to let go.

In this way, faith and hope are intertwined. Faith is the trust we have in God now, and in the present, while hope is the expectation of what that faith will lead to in the future. Both are essential to navigating life's challenges, and both are gifts from God. There have been many moments when hope felt elusive, when the weight of life's burdens seemed too heavy to bear. But even in those times, faith remained, a constant reminder that no matter what, God is in control.

In today's world, expressions of faith and spirituality are as diverse as the cultures and belief systems that exist. People are constantly seeking answers to life's questions and looking for ways to connect with something greater than themselves. However, the paths they take can vary widely. Some turn to organized religions, while others seek out more individualized or even secular forms of spirituality. These expressions of faith cross all cultural and geographic boundaries, and new spiritual movements or practices seem to arise regularly, each offering its own version of peace, fulfillment, and meaning.

Yet, amid this diversity, I find it essential to return to the foundations of what true faith is according to the Bible. While there is value in recognizing and respecting different cultural expressions, we cannot ignore the truth that God reveals in His Word. According to Scripture, faith is a gift from God. It isn't something we can manufacture or earn through human effort. Romans 3:11 reminds us that "There is none who understands, there is none who seeks for God" on their own. God, in His mercy, draws people to Christ and gives them the ability to believe. This is further illustrated in Romans 9:16, which states, "So then it does not depend on the man who wills or the man who runs, but on God who has mercy."

This divine gift of faith is something that transcends human understanding. The natural mind struggles to comprehend it. As 1 Corinthians 2:14 says, "A natural man does not accept the things of the Spirit of God, for they are foolishness to him; and he cannot understand them, because they are spiritually appraised." Faith is something that God graciously reveals to believers, as seen when Jesus tells Peter, "Blessed are you, Simon Barjona, because flesh and blood did not reveal this to you, but My Father who is in heaven" (Matthew 16:17). Faith, then, is not simply one option among many spiritual paths—it is the lifeline that God provides to bring us into a relationship with Him.

It's clear that faith, as defined in the Bible, is not complex, though today's culture often makes it appear elusive or difficult to grasp. Modern society offers countless alternatives and distractions, sometimes making it seem as though faith is just another product to be consumed, another philosophy to be tried out. But true faith is straightforward: it is a gift, freely given by God, and it leads us to peace, hope, and salvation through Jesus Christ.

While observing others during times of hardship, one of the most pressing questions I've faced is "How do people without faith cope with the struggles of life?" Many of my friends, who do not have a saving knowledge of God, often face challenges with little or no solid foundation to fall back on. They strive to endure through sheer willpower or turn to temporary fixes, such as medication or distractions, to numb the pain. While this may offer short-term relief, it is not the lasting peace and comfort that comes from faith in Jesus.

I've witnessed how people, without the grounding of faith, often find themselves endlessly searching for hope, yet struggling to find a sense of meaning in their suffering. They grind away at life, desperate for answers, but the answers they find are fleeting. In contrast, the hope and peace that come from knowing Jesus offers something beyond just temporary comfort. It is a hope rooted in the eternal promises of God—promises that endure beyond our immediate circumstances. While various forms of spirituality or religious rituals in different cultures can provide moments of solace, only faith in God offers true and lasting peace.

Scripture offers numerous assurances of this peace. Philippians 4:7 speaks of "the peace of God, which surpasses all understanding," a peace that guards our hearts and minds in Christ Jesus. It is this peace that has sustained me through the darkest of times. When faced with adversity, I no longer feel the need to rely solely on myself or the solutions the world offers. Instead, I trust in the unshakable foundation of my faith in Christ.

In times of hardship, I've found that certain spiritual practices are particularly helpful in keeping my heart anchored in faith. When faced with struggles, my first response is always to pray more—to spend time talking to God, sharing my fears and doubts with Him, and asking for His guidance and peace. Prayer has a way of shifting my perspective from my immediate worries to the broader reality of God's presence and His plan.

Another practice that has become a cornerstone of my faith journey is reading the Scriptures more frequently during times of difficulty. The Bible is filled with promises that remind me of God's faithfulness. Passages like Isaiah 41:10, which says, "Fear not, for I am with you; be not dismayed, for I am your God. I will strengthen you, I will help you," provide comfort when life feels overwhelming. Scripture grounds me in the truth of who God is and helps me remember that my struggles are not without purpose.

Additionally, leaning on my trusted circle of friends and fellow believers has been a great source of strength. In moments when my faith feels weak, their encouragement and support often remind me not to rely solely on my understanding but to trust in God's plan. Proverbs 27:17 says, "As iron sharpens iron, so one person sharpens another." In difficult seasons, the wisdom and counsel of those who walk with me in faith have been invaluable.

Ultimately, I've learned that faith is not about having all the answers but about trusting in the One who does. It's about being able to say, "I don't understand this right now, but I trust that God does." In moments of uncertainty, prayer, Scripture, and community have been the pillars that hold me up and guide me through.

Faith isn't always easy, but it is always worth it. In every trial, God has shown me that He is faithful.

When facing impending struggles, I often find myself aware of the dark clouds gathering on the horizon. These moments can be unsettling, and our human instinct is to brace for impact. It's almost automatic; fear and anxiety begin to bubble up, prompting us to react defensively. However, in these trying times, I've learned that our first response should be to seek God. When I sense the storm approaching, I remind myself to ask God for the hope that may not yet be visible to me. This act of seeking helps shift my focus from the chaos around me to the calmness of His presence.

By consciously redirecting my emotions toward God instead of allowing them to spiral inwardly, I find that I can navigate life's challenges with greater joy and peace. It's a daily practice to cultivate this mindset, and it requires intention. When we lean on God rather than our own understanding, we allow His strength to guide us through the struggle, creating a space where personal agency and faith can coexist harmoniously.

Faith serves as a powerful catalyst in decision-making, especially during adversity. It instills a deep-seated assurance that, despite the challenges we face, victory is attainable. When

I speak of faith, I'm referring to the trust I place in Jesus, who embodies the ultimate source of reliability. In moments of trial, I reflect on this trust. If my anchor is in Christ, who is more trustworthy than any human being, then I can confidently move forward.

In contrast, relying on friends, co-workers, or even well-meaning pastors can lead to complications, as humans are inherently fallible. Our trust in Jesus equips us with the knowledge that we have divine resources at our disposal—strength, wisdom, and peace—that are far beyond what we can muster on our own. This faith fuels hope and empowers action, allowing me to tackle challenges head-on rather than shrink back in fear. The assurance that I'm not alone in my struggles fosters a resilience that becomes a source of strength for myself and others.

The interplay between faith and personal agency creates a robust framework for developing a resilient mindset. Our emotions, while powerful, can sometimes lead us astray if not anchored in faith. However, when we consciously place our faith at the forefront, we invite a transformative change in how we respond to adversity.

Trusting in the Creator of the universe, who knows me intimately, allows me to confront my challenges with confidence. This divine trust encourages me to embrace my human nature while keeping my faith aligned with my actions. By putting faith ahead of emotions, I am reminded that I possess the ability to overcome even the most daunting obstacles. It's this act of obedience—choosing to trust over despair—that brings about the resilience we all seek.

This journey toward resilience is not about denying our humanity or the weight of our emotions; rather, it's about acknowledging them while placing our trust in a higher power. It's the recognition that we are human, and in our frailty, we find strength through faith. Embracing this synergy between faith and personal agency can ultimately lead us to a more joyful existence, even amid struggles, as we learn to see challenges as opportunities for growth and transformation.

In moments of adversity, our instinctual reactions can lead us down unproductive paths. I've seen this firsthand in the lives of others who, without the anchor of faith, struggle to navigate their challenges effectively. Relying solely on human reasoning can cloud judgment and complicate decisions. My own experience has shown me that faith—specifically, the unwavering trust I place in Jesus Christ—serves as a pivotal point during life's crossroads.

Imagine standing at a fork in the road, where one path appears longer and fraught with obstacles, while the other seems shorter and easier. If faith is the compass guiding my journey, it becomes clear that regardless of the path's length or difficulty, having faith infuses hope and purpose into my decisions. It illuminates the way forward, making each struggle more manageable and instilling a sense of direction that transcends mere human understanding.

Faith is not just a vague belief; it is a deeply rooted conviction that shapes my choices. It provides a framework for discerning right from wrong and encourages me to seek God's will. When I place my decisions in His hands, I find myself more equipped to tackle challenges with resilience and grace.

One of the most profound decisions in my life is the act of writing this book. What began as a simple story titled "The Struggle" has blossomed into an exploration of faith and resilience across twelve chapters. I recall the initial hesitation—wondering if this was indeed what God wanted me to pursue. After months of contemplation, it was faith that ultimately spurred me into action.

As I penned down each chapter, I sensed God guiding my thoughts, shaping my narrative, and refining my voice. The process of writing became an act of obedience—a response to a call that, at times, felt daunting yet deeply fulfilling. It's essential to be discerning when speaking about divine guidance. Many claim to hear from God, but it is crucial to approach such assertions with humility and clarity. However, the transformation I've experienced throughout this writing journey is undeniable. The faith that propelled me into this project continues to influence its outcome, not only by enriching the content but also by deepening my connection to the message I wish to convey.

Placing my trust in something greater than myself has brought immense comfort, especially during turbulent times. Knowing that I can lean on God instills a profound sense of assurance that ultimately, everything will be okay. This reassurance transcends life's fleeting circumstances and extends into the realm of death. The peace that comes from faith soothes my mental and emotional turmoil, grounding me when the storms of life threaten to overwhelm.

Faith is not just a comfort; it is a powerful antidote to anxiety and despair. It has a remarkable ability to quiet my worries, allowing my emotional well-being to flourish in the midst of chaos. By placing my trust in God, I can navigate life's challenges with a renewed perspective, recognizing that I am not alone in my struggles.

I firmly believe in the importance of engaging with the Scriptures personally. Rather than relying solely on the interpretations of others, I encourage everyone to dive deep into the Word of God for themselves. This approach fosters personal growth and abundant hope. Throughout my journey, I have been blessed with spiritual mentors who have offered invaluable guidance during difficult times.

Pastor Larry Upchurch instilled in me the importance of leading with a passion for God, encouraging me to uplift and develop others in their faith. Pastor Jeff Jones taught me humility, emphasizing the necessity of seeking God during struggles. Pastor Danny Jarmon reassured me that it's acceptable to stumble; failure doesn't negate God's plans, and getting back up is part of the journey. Pastor Bill Rose reminded me of my humanity, affirming that it's okay to be a work in progress. Pastors Jeff and Jami Allensworth challenged me to expand my understanding of God, teaching me that He cannot be confined to the small box I had created for Him.

These leaders, through their wisdom and support, have profoundly shaped my spiritual journey. They have helped me grow not only as a man of faith but also as a better husband and father. Their teachings have provided a foundation that supports me through various struggles, equipping me with the tools I need to confront life's challenges head-on.

During my time with the ministry In His Wakes in 2006 and 2007, I encountered many individuals grappling with their struggles. We organized outings to the lake, where young people could escape their difficulties, learn to waterski, or even experience the water for the first time. One poignant event at Rodgers Lake in South Carolina stands out in my memory. I had read about three boys in the newspaper who had been removed from their home under tragic circumstances; one had a broken arm, while the others bore visible injuries.

On the day of the event, as the vans rolled in, I immediately recognized one boy with a broken arm, accompanied by his two brothers. They clung together, a visible testament to their bond amidst hardship. Later, as I shared my story with the group, I was struck by the realization that these were the same boys from the newspaper article. Despite not knowing their full story, I understood that sharing my hope in Jesus with them could make a difference. I wanted them to leave knowing that, if I could find hope, so could they.

That day, I witnessed firsthand how faith could illuminate the darkest paths, providing light in places overshadowed by despair. My message resonated with those boys, serving as a reminder that hope exists even in the most challenging circumstances.

Faith weaves a thread of love through all circumstances, infusing hope into every struggle. It acts as a beacon for those who feel lost, guiding them toward a future filled with possibility. I've observed how faith fosters resilience in others, encouraging them to persevere despite their challenges. It provides a sense of community, reminding us that we are not alone in our trials.

Time and again, I have witnessed individuals find strength in their faith that allows them to rise above their difficulties. Whether it's through acts of kindness, shared prayers, or supportive words, faith ignites a fire of hope that empowers people to keep moving forward. In my experience, faith transforms not only the individual but also the community, creating a ripple effect of hope and love that can uplift and inspire those around us.

CHAPTER TEN

EVIL IN THE STRUGGLE

In times of deep struggle, the presence of evil forces can feel overwhelming. But what exactly is evil? How do these forces manifest when we are at our lowest, grappling with the most profound challenges? In this chapter, we explore the different definitions of evil and how they interact with human suffering. Through real-life examples, personal stories, and reflections on scripture, we hope to uncover the complex relationship between evil, human behavior, and divine will.

Evil is not a one-dimensional concept. It takes many forms, each influencing our lives in different ways. One of the most basic types is natural evil, which includes phenomena that occur independently of human actions—such as natural disasters, diseases, and catastrophic events like earthquakes or pandemics. These events, while devastating, are often seen as part of the world's natural order, even if they lead to immense suffering.

Then, there is a moral evil, perhaps the most tangible in human experience. It manifests in behaviors such as greed, pride, lust, hatred, and sinful anger. Romans 3:9-23 and Mark 7:20-23 speak directly to this form of evil, showing how the human heart can be swayed by wickedness. Moral evil is the result of our choices and actions, driven by our sinful nature. In times of struggle, this evil becomes more pronounced, whether through our own actions or the influence of others around us.

Lastly, there is supernatural evil, which refers to forces beyond the natural world—namely, demons and the army of Satan. Though often given undue credit, these forces do play a role in the spiritual warfare that affects our lives. But as humans, we tend to blame the supernatural more than we should. Often, the moral evils we succumb to—pride, greed, lust—are more than enough to cause destruction in our lives without any interference from demonic forces.

In times of personal struggle, moral evils, particularly pride and hatred, are the most visible. They cloud our judgment, push us to make rash decisions, and can lead to greater destruction in our lives. Supernatural evil, while real, does not always need to intervene when human nature alone can create enough chaos.

Consider the story of my friend, who battled depression for years. He sought help through therapy, and conversations with friends, yet found no solace. Eventually, he turned to drugs as an escape. The drugs, while temporarily masking his pain, only deepened his sense of hopelessness. His struggle ended in tragedy when he took his own life.

Was this the work of moral evil, natural evil, or supernatural forces? His addiction may have started as an attempt to cope with the pain of depression—a natural evil, if you will—but as the drug use escalated, it gave way to the moral evils of escapism, denial, and self-destruction. The root cause may have been depression, but the consequences were a mixture of human choices and spiritual struggle.

Some might claim it was the devil's influence, but often we give the devil too much credit for the things we, as flawed humans, can create on our own. Depression, addiction, and ultimately suicide—can arise from the intersection of natural and moral evils, without the need for any supernatural involvement.

But the most significant real-life example of encountering evil lies in the story of Jesus. In Acts 2:22-24, God allowed the ultimate evil—the betrayal and crucifixion of His son—to unfold as part of His divine plan. Sinners, acting in their own moral evil, carried out this act, but it was predestined for a higher purpose. God used their evil to demonstrate His justice and mercy, a powerful reminder that even the greatest acts of human wickedness can serve a divine purpose.

Without this act of evil, where would humanity be today? It's a question worth reflecting on. God allowed this evil to manifest for His glory, and as Romans 9:20-23 teaches, He uses both mercy and wrath to bring about His will.

For many, including myself, encounters with evil can be deeply personal and transformative. Growing up, I faced an evil far more intimate than any external force—a man who tortured me and my siblings both physically and mentally. For years, I harbored a deep hatred for him. I wanted nothing more than to see him suffer, to witness his downfall as a form of retribution for all the pain he caused us.

But through the grace of God, my perspective shifted. Over time, I began to hope that he would find Jesus, even if only for a moment. I imagined how different he might have been had he experienced just a fraction of the mercy and love I found in Christ. While I still carry the scars of his actions, I now wish for his salvation rather than his demise.

This transformation was not easy, nor did it happen overnight. It was a journey of letting go of the desire for vengeance and embracing the idea that even the worst of us can be redeemed. This personal encounter with evil helped me to understand that while God allows evil to exist, He also provides the tools for overcoming it—namely, forgiveness, mercy, and grace.

Evil, in all its forms, has a place in this world. Whether natural, moral, or supernatural, it is allowed to exist by God's will. As Isaiah 45:5-7 tells us, God creates both light and darkness, peace and calamity. He allows evil to unfold, but always for a greater purpose.

In our struggles, we often wrestle with the presence of evil, questioning why it exists and how we can overcome it. The truth is, that evil serves a purpose, even when we don't fully understand it. It challenges us, tests us, and ultimately leads us back to God. Whether through personal experiences, like the abuse I endured, or larger cosmic battles like the crucifixion of Christ, evil is part of the human experience. But it is not without hope. For in every struggle, there is the possibility of redemption, healing, and growth.

As we examine the role of evil in our lives, I encourage you to reflect on your own encounters with darkness. How have they shaped you? And how might you, too, find grace in the midst of the struggle?

It can be difficult to recognize when evil forces or negative influences are impacting our lives, particularly because they often present themselves in subtle, almost unnoticeable ways. However, there are certain signs that individuals can look for that may indicate they are being affected. The first and most essential step is being rooted in the guidance of Biblical Scriptures. The Word of God provides clarity and direction, helping to expose evil for what it truly is. When we distance ourselves from God's teachings, we become more susceptible to the lure of worldly influences that can lead us astray.

One of the clearest indicators that we are being affected by evil forces is a shift in our mindset or behavior. Feelings of overwhelming negativity, constant anger, envy, or the inability to find peace in daily life are often signs that something darker may be at play. When moral compasses begin to falter and actions that once seemed unthinkable start to feel justified, that's when it becomes clear we're treading dangerous ground. Evil doesn't always appear as some grand, overt force; it often works subtly, weaving its way into our thoughts and decisions, steering us toward self-destructive habits.

Social media, for example, is one of the most prevalent platforms for negative influences today. On the surface, it may seem harmless or even entertaining, but the underlying effects it has on our minds and souls can be profound. The constant comparison to others, the desire for validation, and the distraction from more meaningful pursuits are all ways in which these platforms can subtly erode our sense of self-worth and spiritual grounding. In many ways, it's a tool for evil, as it capitalizes on human weaknesses—vanity, pride, greed, and envy.

Supernatural evil, though very real, often works in conjunction with our own sinful nature, exploiting these vulnerabilities. In today's world, the barrage of information and images we are exposed to through various forms of media can heighten the presence of these forces. We are more easily distracted from God's Word and lured into the destructive cycles of consumption, comparison, and indulgence. The battle for our souls has moved from physical spaces into digital ones, and it's easy to fall into these traps without even realizing it.

One of the most effective ways to combat these negative influences is to be vigilant and proactive in our spiritual lives. Diving deeper into the Scriptures and asking for God's guidance is crucial. Regular prayer, meditation on God's Word, and surrounding oneself with a strong community of believers provide the armor needed to fight against these forces. It's important to recognize when feelings of anxiety, depression, or anger seem to dominate, and instead of letting these emotions fester, turn to God in those moments of weakness. The Bible reminds us that evil seeks to destroy, but it also tells us that God is always near, waiting to provide comfort and strength when we seek it.

Transparency is another vital component. Many times, people hide their struggles, unwilling to admit that they are being influenced by something negative or evil. This secrecy only allows the force to grow stronger. When we are open about our struggles, either with God or with others who can help, we are less likely to fall victim to these influences. It's in isolation that evil thrives, feeding on shame and guilt.

The mental health crisis we are facing today is, in part, a reflection of this hidden battle. Many are overwhelmed by negative influences, whether they stem from societal pressures, personal failures, or a loss of spiritual grounding. The Bible offers not just spiritual guidance but practical wisdom, reminding us that in our times of struggle, we are not alone. There is a way out, and that way begins by turning to God's Word and finding strength in Him.

As I've often told myself, "If I spent half as much time in the Bible as I do on social media, I would be a much stronger person in Christ." This realization comes from acknowledging that the more time we invest in God's Word, the less influence the world has over us. The more we align our lives with His teachings, the easier it becomes to resist the subtle lures of evil.

By immersing ourselves in Scripture, we develop the discernment needed to recognize when negative influences are creeping into our lives. This allows us to react quickly, turning to prayer and the Word of God before the struggle deepens. Ultimately, the key is maintaining a strong, unwavering connection with God. In doing so, we arm ourselves against the forces of evil, whether they come in the form of moral decay, supernatural influence, or simply the everyday temptations that surround us.

The strategies to combat evil influences may seem straightforward in theory but can be challenging to implement in the heat of life's struggles. It's often only when we find ourselves deep in a crisis that we turn to God for help when in truth, the best strategy is to be vigilant and proactive long before the struggle even begins. Being mindful of what we allow into our minds and souls is key. What we watch, listen to, and expose ourselves to daily has a profound impact on our spiritual health. Social media, in particular, plays a significant role in this. Its dominance in our lives—and especially in the lives of our children—cannot be ignored. It's not only a platform for connection but also a breeding ground for envy, anger, and destructive behavior.

One of the most effective strategies is to monitor and limit what we consume through media. It's easy to react impulsively, to post a hateful comment, or to engage in negativity online when we feel attacked or frustrated. But this is exactly where evil gains a foothold. The enemy works through these moments of vulnerability, fueling the fire of our anger and pride. Instead of reacting emotionally, we need to practice self-control and rely on God's wisdom to guide our actions. Staying grounded in His Word, even if it's just reading a verse each day, helps build spiritual resilience. This consistent intake of Scripture serves as a daily reminder of God's presence and power in our lives, giving us strength when the storms of life arise.

Prayer is another crucial element in battling these negative forces. Prayer connects us directly to God, offering a line of communication to seek His guidance and strength in times of weakness. When we see struggles on the horizon—and they will surely come—prayer becomes our anchor. It reminds us that we are not fighting alone and that God is with us in every battle, ready to give us the tools we need to resist evil and rise above adversity.

But it's not just about prayer and Scripture reading. Personal responsibility plays an enormous role in overcoming adversity and resisting negative influences. We must take ownership of our lives, decisions, and actions. Setting boundaries is essential. Limiting contact with people who consistently bring negativity into your life and avoiding places or situations that may tempt you into sin are important steps. This extends to the virtual world as well—social media can easily become a source of negativity, so learning to limit its impact on your mental and spiritual well-being is vital.

Self-awareness is key. Pay attention to your mental state and emotions on a day-to-day basis. Are you feeling frustrated, envious, or anxious? These feelings often open the door to negative influences if left unchecked. By identifying these emotions early on, we can take proactive steps to address them, rather than allowing them to fester and lead us down a destructive path. It's not enough to merely react to struggles as they come; we must actively prepare for them by maintaining a mindset rooted in faith and responsibility.

Taking charge of your own struggles also requires a significant shift in mindset. Instead of adopting a victim mentality—where external circumstances or evil forces are always to blame—recognize that you have the power to choose how you respond to adversity. This doesn't mean denying the existence of evil or its influence, but rather acknowledging that with God's help, you have the strength to resist and rise above it. By shifting your mindset from one of helplessness to one of empowerment, you reclaim control over your spiritual journey.

Ultimately, staying anchored in God's Word, setting healthy boundaries, and maintaining a proactive and responsible mindset are the most effective ways to resist the evil forces and negative influences that inevitably arise during times of struggle. Life will present challenges, but by remaining vigilant and rooted in faith, we are equipped to face them with strength and grace.

Resilience is the ability to bounce back from adversity, and it plays a crucial role in helping individuals withstand the influence of evil forces. Each struggle we face and overcome strengthens our capacity to handle future challenges, building resilience step by step. When we emerge from a difficult situation with a positive outcome, we not only gain experience but also develop a deeper understanding of ourselves and the world around us. This accumulation of resilience equips us to face the next battle, though each struggle has its own unique complexity, which means the tools we've gained from one experience may not always apply to the next.

The presence of evil forces in our struggles can, paradoxically, become opportunities for growth. As we navigate through adversity, we often make mistakes, but these mistakes are where we learn the most. The process of recognizing and correcting our errors strengthens our resilience, enabling us to persevere even when the odds seem overwhelming. Over time, resilience nurtures a new level of mental fortitude, allowing us to better understand our emotional responses and behavior patterns in the face of difficulty. It's a learning curve that reshapes us, not just physically, but mentally and spiritually.

I've been married for forty years, and during that time, I've made countless mistakes that could have easily destroyed my marriage. I often tell people, "I've done everything possible to mess this marriage up," but through it all, my wife, Sweet Lisa, has been the resilient one. She has consistently fought for us, for our marriage, and for me. No matter how dark the situation became, no matter how much the evil forces of pride, anger, or temptation tried to tear us apart, she held on. Her resilience became our saving grace.

Lisa recognized that real love is a foundation for resilience. It's love that gave her the strength to keep fighting even when it seemed hopeless, and it's that same love that ultimately helped us withstand the evil forces that tried to destroy our relationship. She didn't fight against me; she fought for me. That's the key—having people in your corner who are willing to fight with you, not against you. Resilience doesn't develop in isolation. It's built within the context of relationships, faith, and a willingness to keep pushing forward, even when the struggle seems endless.

Through Lisa's example, I've come to understand that love is not just a feeling; it's a powerful tool that builds resilience. It defeats the evil forces that seek to break us down. When you're surrounded by love and support, you find the strength to rise above the negativity and keep moving forward.

Societal and environmental factors play a significant role in shaping the presence and impact of evil influences during times of struggle. The people we surround ourselves with, the communities we engage in, and the media we consume can either lift us up or pull us down into darker places. In the midst of a personal battle, the environment you immerse yourself in can mean the difference between life and death—not just physically, but mentally and spiritually as well.

We live in a fallen state of humanity, where death is inevitable, but evil forces often seek to accelerate that destruction. These forces thrive in chaos, addiction, and isolation, aiming to strip away all that is good and meaningful. In many cases, it's not enough to just fight the inner battle; you must also reassess your external environment. For example, if you're struggling with addiction, whether to drugs or other harmful behaviors, staying in the same toxic surroundings will only lead to relapse and further despair. Radical changes are often required to create a space for healing and recovery. This means cutting off relationships that feed into the cycle of negativity and rebuilding your life in an environment that promotes growth, positivity, and accountability.

The influence of social media cannot be underestimated here. When you are in the middle of a struggle, social media often offers nothing of value. In fact, it frequently exacerbates the problem by fueling comparison, envy, and unhealthy distractions. It can amplify the voices of negativity that already haunt your thoughts. The curated lives and opinions of others can make your struggles feel insurmountable, leading to feelings of inadequacy and hopelessness. That's why, in times of adversity, it's crucial to step away from platforms that do more harm than good.

You are a product of your surroundings. The people you choose to keep close, the places you frequent, and the things you engage with all shape who you are. If your environment is filled with toxic influences, that negativity will seep into your choices, your mindset, and your overall outlook on life. Likewise, if you surround yourself with positive, supportive individuals and environments that encourage your growth, you will have a much better chance of overcoming the evil forces in your struggle.

Ultimately, your choices and your relationships are interconnected. The decisions you make will influence the people you draw into your life, and those relationships, in turn, will affect your future decisions. If you want to defeat the evil in your struggle, you have to be intentional about your environment. Seek out spaces and people who nurture your resilience and strength, and be willing to walk away from anything or anyone that pulls you into negativity.

When you ignore or succumb to negative influences, the consequences can be severe and far-reaching. Your struggles will persist, cycling back into your life, often becoming more intense and destructive over time. Negative influences, whether they come from toxic relationships, destructive habits, or harmful environments, will continue to pull you down if left unchecked. Radical action is sometimes necessary to break free, even if that means making difficult decisions like ending a long-term friendship that has become toxic.

It's not easy to let go of things that have been a part of your life for a long time, but the price of holding on to negativity is even greater. Continuing to ignore these harmful influences will lead to being stuck in a dark, unhealthy place, repeating the same struggles over and over again. The world has a way of finding our weaknesses, and evil forces will always try to exploit those vulnerabilities. That's why it's crucial to surround yourself with people who respect the boundaries you set and genuinely support your well-being. When others respect your boundaries, it's a sign they respect you—and that's a key factor in building a life of resilience and strength.

When you do give in to negative influences, there's still an opportunity to learn from the experience. Often, the hardest lessons come from our darkest moments, and it's in those moments we can grow the most. Understanding where we went wrong, acknowledging the weaknesses that led us astray, and taking ownership of our choices can lead to personal growth and greater wisdom. Every failure is an opportunity to rebuild, and every mistake is a chance to develop a stronger sense of self-awareness.

Support systems, whether they are friends, family, or mentors, play a critical role in helping individuals navigate their struggles and combat the evil forces they face. No one can do life alone, and having a trusted circle of people who will stand with you through tough times is invaluable. As mentioned in previous discussions, transparency is a vital part of this process. When you are open and honest about what you're going through, your support system can step in and help you. But if you keep your struggles to yourself, internalizing your pain and hiding your emotions, no one will know how to help.

Being transparent isn't easy. It requires trust and vulnerability, and it's something many people—including myself—struggle with. But it's essential. The Bible tells us that our battles aren't just against physical things but also against spiritual forces. Evil is persistent, always seeking to tear us down, whether it's through natural, moral, or supernatural means. That's why we need others to help us in our journey. Asking for help isn't a sign of weakness—it's a recognition that we're all in this together, and none of us can fight these battles alone. The world needs you, and the people around you want to help you succeed.

In reflecting on the concept of evil in our struggles, it's important to remember that resilience is not just a nice idea; it's a necessity. Resilience is the ability to keep going, to bounce back after every setback, and to never give up, no matter how tough things get. Developing resilience means cultivating a mindset of victory—believing that no matter what, you're still here, and you're still fighting. It's about embracing the idea that, though life will have its dark moments, it will also have times of great joy and beauty.

Faith plays a huge role in resilience. Trusting that there is hope, even in the most difficult times, gives us the strength to keep going. Life is short, and we have much to accomplish in the time we're given. So we need to make the most of it, doing our best every day and never giving up. Even in times of struggle, we can find ways to make the world a more beautiful place, to bring light into the darkness. Be the one who makes a difference in someone else's life, and in doing so, you'll find that you've built a life of resilience and meaning.

CHAPTER ELEVEN

BRINGING HOPE AND DISCOVERING VICTORY IN THE STRUGGLE

In the midst of life's relentless challenges, the stories of hope resonate like a distant bell, echoing the truth that even in darkness, light can break through. Why do these narratives strike such a profound chord in the hearts of those wrestling with their own battles? The answer lies in our intrinsic design as human beings: hope is the key to facing any struggle. It fuels our resilience, ignites our spirits, and, at times, is all we have left to cling to.

Isaiah 40:31 beautifully encapsulates this truth: "But those who hope in the Lord will renew their strength. They will soar on wings like eagles; they will run and not grow weary, they will walk and not be faint." In these words, we find the promise that hope renews not just our spirit but also our very essence, propelling us toward the possibility of triumph even when the path seems fraught with peril.

Consider the powerful journey of individuals who have faced their breaking points yet chose resilience over defeat. The story of Job stands as a profound testament to this struggle. Job, a man of unwavering faith, endured unimaginable loss and suffering. His friends, in their well-meaning attempts to comfort him, often added to his pain by questioning his righteousness. Yet, through it all, Job remained steadfast. His story illustrates that even in the depths of despair when the soul feels most broken, one can choose to trust in a sovereign God.

Despite the chaos that enveloped him, Job's resilience stemmed from an internal strength—a faith that refused to waver in the face of adversity. As he grappled with profound questions of justice and suffering, he ultimately learned to bow before God's wisdom, trusting that there was purpose in his pain. This brings us to a crucial understanding: victory in the struggle is not always marked by tangible achievements but often by personal growth and inner transformation. Job emerged from his trials not with trophies but with a deeper understanding of God's grace and a renewed hope that even in suffering, there lies the potential for profound personal evolution.

As we navigate our own struggles, we may not always see immediate signs of victory. Instead, we often experience a more subtle, yet significant, shift within ourselves. The trials we endure produce patience, character, and, ultimately, hope. This hope becomes a lifeline, a flickering light in the darkest of nights, reminding us that our journey is not in vain. It urges us to focus on God's promises, assuring us that He does not desire to harm us but rather to bring us peace and joy.

Yet, maintaining a sense of purpose amid unending struggles can feel insurmountable. It is in these moments that hope becomes our greatest ally. It whispers to us that we are not mere victims of fate, but beloved children of a faithful God who sees our pain and walks beside us. Even when we cannot understand our circumstances, we can trust in the greater narrative of love and redemption woven through our lives.

Stories of hope, like that of Job, remind us that we are not alone. They show us that hope is the heartbeat of resilience, propelling us forward even when the road is steep. Each struggle, while difficult, offers the opportunity for inner transformation. As we hold onto hope, we find not only a way to endure but also the promise of peace that comes after the storm.

In the face of overwhelming adversity, stories of resilience shine brightly, reminding us that even in the darkest moments, hope can serve as our guiding light. One such profound narrative comes from my own childhood, an experience that shaped not only my understanding of struggle but also my capacity for hope.

I vividly recall a time when my brother, Mike, and I were left at an off-grid daycare, a place that soon became a backdrop for our trials. We were just four and five years old, innocent yet caught in a world that didn't seem to care for our well-being. One of our worst experiences was being locked in a dark closet—a cramped space where light rarely penetrated, and time seemed to stretch endlessly.

Inside that closet, we huddled together, the air thick with uncertainty. I would often curl up, resting my head on my knees, my heart heavy with fear and confusion. Mike, a year older and my steadfast companion would sit on the opposite side. Our only comfort lay in each other's presence. I would ask, "Mike, are you there?" and he would respond, "Yes, I'm here." It was a small reassurance amidst the suffocating darkness.

In those hours of confinement, we learned to create our own light. We imagined building a fire—not just for warmth but as a symbol of hope. "Get the fire going because I'm cold," Mike would say, and together, we would envision flames illuminating our confined space. The act of imagining that fire became a necessity, a lifeline that sustained us through the isolation.

As we played this mental game, I stumbled upon something etched into the wall: "Keep the fire going; never let it go out. Fan the flames, and you will make it." The inscription bore a signature that seemed to leap out at me—HOPE. It struck me profoundly; this wasn't just a message for us but for all those who had been confined to this darkness before us. It was a reminder that even in despair, hope existed.

My role in that closet was to nurture that flame of hope. Though I was small and often overwhelmed, I found strength in knowing that I could keep our spirits alive, if only through imagination. Mike and I worked together, each playing our part: he provided the encouragement, and I tended to the flames. This collaboration became a metaphor for our lives; even in the depths of struggle, we could rely on each other to ignite the light of hope.

Emerging from that closet, eyes squinting in the bright light of day, I realized this experience was merely the beginning of a longer journey. Each day presented new challenges, yet the lessons learned in that dark space remained with me. They taught me that hope is not a passive state but an active pursuit, requiring effort and intention.

This narrative echoes the wisdom found in Scripture. Romans 5:3-5 reminds us, "We also have joy with our troubles, because we know that these troubles produce patience. And patience produces character, and character produces hope." In our struggles, we often uncover a resilience we never knew we possessed, a reminder that we are not victims of circumstance but participants in a grander narrative of growth and redemption.

As I reflect on my journey and that of many others who have faced their own darkness, it becomes clear: hope is a powerful force. It not only inspires us to endure but also guides us toward victory. Through adversity, we learn to fan the flames of our spirit, nurturing the light that can illuminate even the darkest of paths.

Cultivating Hope

In the tapestry of life, the threads of hope and perseverance are woven through our most challenging experiences, illuminating the path toward growth and transformation. When faced with adversity, cultivating hope is not just beneficial; it is essential. Here, we explore practical strategies that can empower individuals to harness hope, fostering resilience in their lives.

1. Faith as the Foundation: At the heart of hope lies faith. Trusting in a higher power, particularly in Jesus, can anchor us during turbulent times. This faith instills a belief that no matter how dire the circumstances, there is a promise of light and eventual relief.

2. Prayer and Reflection: Engaging in prayer offers solace and connection. It allows us to pour out our fears and doubts, often revealing a glimmer of hope amid chaos. This conversation with God reassures us that we are not alone, and that divine light shines even in our darkest moments.

3. Building a Supportive Circle: Sharing struggles with trusted friends or family creates a network of understanding and empathy. It's crucial to connect with those who genuinely care, rather than seeking validation through social media. Open conversations can relieve the burden of isolation, preventing internalized pain from spiraling into destructive patterns.

4. Therapy as a Tool for Healing: Professional support can provide invaluable perspective. Finding a therapist who resonates with you can help align thoughts and emotions, fostering clarity and peace. While not all therapists will fit every individual, the right guidance can offer a renewed outlook on life.

5. Practice Self-Care: Caring for your mental, emotional, and physical health is vital in maintaining perseverance. Simple acts—like breathing exercises, journaling, or engaging in creative hobbies—can ground you and provide moments of respite amidst the storm.

Perseverance is defined as the steadfastness to endure challenges and setbacks with resilience. It is an essential trait for spiritual growth, as highlighted in biblical passages. For instance, James 1:2-3 encourages us to find joy in trials, asserting that they help cultivate endurance, character, and hope.

To build perseverance:

- Immerse Yourself in Scripture: Grounding yourself in God's promises through the Bible can be a source of strength. Verses like Proverbs 3:5-6 remind us to trust in the Lord rather than relying solely on our understanding.

- Encourage Community Support: Surround yourself with fellow believers who can uplift you. Hebrews 10:24-25 emphasizes the importance of meeting together to encourage one another through life's challenges.

- Reflect on Past Experiences: Each struggle offers lessons. By learning from previous difficulties, we equip ourselves with tools for future challenges. This reflection fosters a mindset that values growth through adversity.

Self-care is crucial in maintaining perseverance. Taking time to nourish your mind and body can prevent burnout and foster resilience. Remember, as you navigate your struggles, you are not just enduring for yourself but also for those who may rely on your strength in the future.

Billy Graham once said, "Patience includes perseverance—the ability to bear up under weariness, strain, and persecution." Trusting in God during these times can lead to a profound sense of victory.

To truly harness the tools of hope and perseverance, it's essential to integrate them into daily life. This could involve:

- Establishing a Routine: Dedicate specific times for prayer, reading Scripture, and connecting with supportive friends. Consistency can reinforce these practices, making them integral to your life.

- Setting Realistic Goals: Break down your struggles into manageable steps. Celebrate small victories along the way, reinforcing a sense of progress and hope.

- Flexibility in Approach: Each struggle is unique. Adapt your methods to suit your evolving circumstances, recognizing that new challenges require new tools and perspectives.

The growth that emerges from perseverance manifests as inner strength, peace, and a joyful countenance. Romans 5:3-5 beautifully illustrates this transformation: "We can rejoice, too, when we run into problems and trials, for we know that they help us develop endurance." This endurance shapes our character and strengthens our hope.

As your perspective shifts, so do your values and relationships. When we view struggles as opportunities for growth, we cultivate healthier connections and make more conscious choices in our interactions.

Ultimately, faith is the cornerstone of perseverance. It is this unwavering trust that can carry individuals through their darkest hours. Countless biblical figures—like Joseph, Moses, and Job—illustrate how faith in God's plan sustains us through trials.

Moreover, personal testimonies abound, showcasing how hope can lead to profound change. As someone who emerged from a cycle of abuse and despair, I know firsthand how investing in relationships and nurturing hope can alter the trajectory of one's life.

As we come to the close of this chapter, it's vital to reflect on the lessons learned through our shared experiences of struggle and triumph. Life is a series of challenges, and how we approach these trials can determine whether they lead to growth or setbacks. I have learned that the key lies in our response—listening to our trusted circle and heeding the voice of God within us. It is through these whispers of hope that we can navigate the murky waters of adversity.

Each struggle is an opportunity for transformation. While the pain is real and can feel overwhelming, it is essential to recognize that we have the power to choose our response. With every setback, we can cultivate a fortified hope that allows us to bounce back, stronger and more resilient than before. Life may throw unexpected curveballs, but as long as we keep swinging, we remain in the game. Each time we rise after a fall, we not only strengthen our resolve but also expand our capacity for hope.

For those of you grappling with feelings of hopelessness, know this: you are not alone. Sometimes, the greatest gift you can offer yourself is simply the assurance that it's okay to share your struggles. I am here for you, just as so many have been there for me. Together, we can create a safe space for open dialogue, free from judgment and expectation.

Remember, hope is not merely a fleeting feeling; it is a gift bestowed upon us through grace. In our darkest moments, it flickers like a distant star, guiding us through the night. Embrace it. Allow hope to be your anchor, grounding you amidst the storms of life. With faith as your foundation and the support of your circle, you can emerge from every struggle transformed, ready to face whatever comes next.

In this journey, may you always find the courage to keep moving forward, knowing that each step is a testament to your resilience. Let hope be the light that leads you through the darkest valleys, reminding you that even in the midst of struggle, victory is within reach.

CHAPTER TWELVE

LIVING FOR HOPE, FAITH, AND SHOWING MERCY IN THE STRUGGLE

I hope by now you have seen the raw reality of the struggles in my life, and in the lives of my friends and family. More than that, I hope you understand that our only true hope is in our Lord and Savior, Jesus Christ. I acknowledge that not everyone will grasp this truth. Many will remain distracted by the world's temptations, clinging to social media, seeking solace in shallow relationships, and relying on well-meaning but misguided advice from those around them.

But for me, it is only my faith that has carried me through the darkest and most difficult times. It is God's mercy that has pulled me out of the depths of despair, time and again. His promises, laid out in His Word, have been the bedrock on which I've built my life. They've provided the hope I needed to keep pushing forward, even when the road ahead seemed impossible.

I wish I could say that I always responded perfectly to the challenges in my life, that I always sought after God's will and trusted fully in His promises. But that hasn't been the case. I've stumbled more times than I can count. I've made choices that were far from His path, decisions that left me broken and lost. Even so, in my darkest moments, there was always a small part of me—sometimes buried deep—that sought after His grace and mercy, even when I didn't realize it.

There was a time in my marriage when I made some terrible decisions, both in my personal relationships and in my ministry. I allowed myself to be led by my own desires, chasing after what seemed right at the time but was actually rooted in pride and the temptations of the world. I convinced myself that I could handle it, that I could save the world on my own terms. But it wasn't long before I found myself in a tailspin, my marriage and ministry on the brink of destruction.

What saved me wasn't my own strength or wisdom—it was the unwavering love of my wife. She fought for me even when I had given up. She believed in the hope and promises of God when I couldn't. It was her faith, and the grace and mercy of God, that restored our marriage and brought healing to us both. What could have ended in ruin became a story of redemption, not because of anything we did, but because of His grace.

None of us are immune to struggle, no matter how long we've walked with God. After more than forty years of marriage, we still face battles, but they are manageable only through His grace, His mercy, and the guiding principles of His Word. The world offers countless distractions—social media, the news, the opinions of others—but none of them provide the lasting hope that God does. It's up to each of us to choose where we invest our time and attention. Do we fill our minds with His truth, or do we allow the world to shape our thinking? It's a choice we must make every day.

God has a way of orchestrating relationships in such a way that they become lifelines of hope, faith, and mercy. That's exactly how it happened with our friends, Ed and Nida. I remember the day Ed called me, asking to meet up. We found ourselves in a parking lot of a coffee shop, and he was searching for something more, something deeper. He wanted to know about God's love and this "salvation" that we often spoke of.

I don't remember every detail of that first conversation, but I know it became the beginning of a journey. For the next twelve weeks, Ed and Nida came to our home, and each week, we tackled different topics that would guide them toward an understanding of faith. As an analyst by profession, Ed's mind was wired for details, logic, and clarity. He needed to grasp all the intricacies of faith, grace, and mercy, according to God's Word. So, we studied diligently—discussing, dissecting, and questioning every concept.

What started as a simple meeting soon became something that transformed not just Ed and Nida, but us as well. Each week, I found myself diving deeper into the Word, studying more thoroughly, knowing that their questions were coming. It was exhilarating, trying to answer the profound questions that Ed and Nida would bring. Ed would pose a tough question, and then Nida would follow with another, and together we navigated the complexities of faith. But in reality, it wasn't complicated at all. God's grace was woven into every meeting, every question, and every discussion.

As we neared the end of our study, I asked them, "Does it all make sense now?" Ed's answer was unforgettable. He said, "Does it make sense? No. Do I believe it? Yes." Nida gave us a nod of agreement, her eyes filled with the same conviction. Those words have stuck with me ever since. Do I understand? No. Do I believe? Yes. That is the transformative power of God's grace. He doesn't call us to fully understand, but simply to believe. To trust that He has everything under control, even when it doesn't make sense to us.

That's what I treasure about the story of Ed and Nida. They were raised with beliefs and values that differed from what God's mercy and grace offer. Yet, through those twelve weeks, they encountered something far greater than understanding—they encountered faith. Are they perfect now? Are we perfect? Of course not. But we continue to grow, knowing that God is with us every step of the way. That brings immense comfort in a world filled with struggles.

Ed and Nida remain dear friends to this day, and we've had the privilege of enjoying life alongside them and their family. That's the beauty of relationships—they are vessels of grace, filled with purpose, and shaped by God's hand. Through His mercy, He brought them to redemption, and through His grace, we continue to journey together.

In the face of adversity, one of the most powerful strategies I've embraced is living with authenticity and transparency. I believe that transparency is the key to clarity, and in any struggle, clarity is what paves the way for victory. Being real and honest, both with yourself and with others, is the core value that can either prolong your struggle or bring you closer to the breakthrough.

No two struggles are alike. Each one is a unique journey with its own set of challenges. But one thing remains constant: the enemy seeks to destroy us, while God leads us to victory. Every adversity has the potential to shape us in a positive direction, even if it's hard to see in the moment.

I don't want to offer a false sense of hope by saying that everything will always turn out okay. Sometimes it doesn't. It all depends on the choices you make during the struggle. It depends on how you respond when the darkness feels overwhelming. I'm not one to say, "Just trust God and everything will be fine." That's not always how it works. Yes, trust in God is essential, but it also requires human effort. It requires us to lean into a faith we may not fully understand, and to keep moving forward, even when it feels impossible.

God is the one who brings that belief into existence. He calls us to step out in faith, even when the path ahead is unclear. Living authentically, admitting our fears and doubts, is part of the journey. It's in those raw, unfiltered moments of honesty that God's grace meets us, guiding us through the adversity. It's through transparency that we begin to see His hand at work, even when the situation seems hopeless.

So, in every struggle I face, I try to live authentically, to be real about my fears and failures. I trust that, in doing so, God will bring clarity, hope, and victory. Not because I have it all figured out, but because He does.

I want to leave you with one core message: always keep hope alive. No matter what life throws at you, hold on to hope. Struggles will come—there's no avoiding them. But I believe these struggles are not arbitrary; they are a part of life's cycle designed to draw us closer to God, our Father, the Creator of the universe.

Some struggles will feel overwhelming, while others might seem more manageable, but each one has a purpose in our journey toward understanding His grace and mercy. The way we rise after each struggle has a profound impact, not only on ourselves but also on the people around us—our families, our friends, and our communities. Every time we face adversity and come out stronger, it breathes new life into our relationships. Even when the outcome isn't what we expected, there is still hope to be found.

It's easy to assume that a negative outcome means failure, but that's not always the case. Just because something didn't turn out the way we wanted, doesn't mean it didn't unfold the way it was meant to. Sometimes, it takes years to fully understand why certain struggles happened or how they shaped our lives. That's the mystery of faith—it often requires patience and trust that everything is unfolding according to God's perfect plan, even when we can't see it in the moment.

To anyone navigating their own struggles right now, I want you to know that hope is real. It's not a distant, unreachable concept—it's right here, even in the hardest of times. The strength to endure these challenges doesn't come from the world, from social media, or from the people who may not have your best interests at heart. Sometimes, you may not even find strength in yourself. But there is a source of unwavering strength: God's Word.

Trust that the outcome of your struggles will be complete, and that it will be in your favor, whatever that might look like. The key to finding hope in the midst of adversity is believing that God is real, that He is sovereign, and that He is in control of your life and the entire universe. There is a force—one that seeks to harm, to destroy, and to distract you—but God's will is greater. He is guiding you through every hardship, and His plans for you are good, even when the road feels difficult.

When you feel weak, turn to the Bible, the ultimate source of hope and strength. God's promises are enduring, and they are the foundation upon which we can stand. Here are a few powerful scriptures that can serve as anchors in your time of need:

- Romans 15:13: *"May the God of hope fill you with all joy and peace in believing, so that by the power of the Holy Spirit you may abound in hope."*

- Psalm 31:24: *"Be strong and take heart, all you who hope in the LORD."*

- Isaiah 40:31: *"But those who hope in the LORD will renew their strength. They will soar on wings like eagles; they will run and not grow weary, they will walk and not be faint."*

- Hebrews 11:1: *"Now faith is confidence in what we hope for and assurance about what we do not see."*

- Jeremiah 29:11: *"For I know the plans I have for you," declares the Lord, "plans to prosper you and not to harm you, plans to give you hope and a future."*

These verses remind us that hope is not just an emotional feeling; it's a deep, abiding trust in God's promises. It's the assurance that no matter how dark the situation may seem, God is working for your good. Even in the waiting, even in the uncertainty, hope is there to sustain you.

So as you face your struggles, remember that you are not alone. God is with you, guiding you, and strengthening you. Let hope be your anchor, and trust that whatever the outcome, it will be part of His perfect plan for your life.

Family can be a tremendous source of support during struggles, but they can also complicate things. Sometimes, they may want you to conform to their expectations or act in a way that saves face, especially when it comes to sensitive issues. This pressure can make the struggle feel even more daunting. To truly cope with any struggle, we must lean on our community—those family members and friends we trust. It's important to recognize that there will always be people on the outside wanting to interfere, but their motives may not align with your best interests. This principle applies to both family and friends; not everyone is meant to be involved in your journey.

When my wife, Lisa, and I found ourselves deep in the struggle to save our marriage, we learned a harsh lesson about the people in our lives. There were those who genuinely cared and wanted to help us navigate our challenges, but there were also others who seemed to relish the idea of watching our marriage dissolve. Some of these were family members, and others were friends. This created a new layer of complexity to our struggle. Not only were we facing external pressures, but there were also individuals close to us who seemed to wish for our downfall.

It was only through our complete transparency with our church family and our trusted friends that we found a path to victory. We emerged stronger, and I can say with confidence that we discovered who our true friends were—those who stood by us in our darkest hours and offered support rather than judgment. I wish I could say that you can always trust those closest to you, but that's not always the case. What we can always trust is that God will provide victory in our struggles. In Him, we find peace and happiness.

In the midst of trials, I have learned the importance of staying in prayer and immersing myself in God's Word. What we read and what we focus on shapes who we are. It's vital to engage with Scripture directly and not rely solely on others to convey its truths. This may sound simple, yet in a world filled with distractions—like social media and the constant barrage of news—it becomes challenging to make room for God in our lives. I often reflect on how, if I could dedicate just a fraction of the time I spend on social media to reading the Bible, I would be transformed.

Our faith is consistently challenged by the enemy of this world. However, as part of the elect, we know we have victory that cannot be taken from us. When we lean on the God of hope, we truly lack nothing.

James 1:2-4 reminds us of this:

"Count it all joy, my brothers, when you meet trials of various kinds, for you know that the testing of your faith produces steadfastness. And let steadfastness have its full effect, that you may be perfect and complete, lacking in nothing."

As I conclude this chapter, I want to encourage you to pursue life with your eyes fixed on God, the ultimate source of hope—the giver of life and the one who instills in you the faith to believe. This belief, rooted in hope, is what you need in your struggles. Hope is not a vague notion; it's a tangible reality that can coexist with pain, sorrow, and even death.

I recall a moment in a restaurant when our server had the phrase "the struggle is real" tattooed on her arm. It struck me as profoundly true. The reality of life includes real struggles, but it is God who brings true life and authentic hope, enabling us to find victory amid all circumstances.

As I leave you with my thoughts on hope, I want to share one of my favorite passages, Jeremiah 29:11:

"For I know the plans I have for you," declares the Lord, "plans to prosper you and not to harm you, plans to give you a hope and a future."

This verse is often viewed as a powerful testament to God's goodness. It serves as encouragement during suffering and a reminder of His control, allowing us to relinquish our worries about the future.

His faithfulness, His promises, and His love resonate deeply with me. Time and again, I've experienced His covenant path, even during moments when I felt unloving, unfaithful, or lacking peace. Through His grace, I am continually being transformed into His likeness, growing in faith, love, and peace. Today, I carry joy, harmony, and a heart filled with praise.

Above all, I desire to be an encouragement to others and to sing an anthem of hope to the Bride. If you're facing pain, hardship, loss, or disappointment, remember that victories can be won, dreams can be realized, and beautiful endings can unfold. God remains the same, yesterday, today, and forever. Because of this, I am filled with encouragement, trusting in His plan for you and for me. Whatever you are experiencing, know that He is right there with you in your struggles.

www.ingramcontent.com/pod-product-compliance
Lightning Source LLC
LaVergne TN
LVHW050817061126
851857LV00012B/851